Spoken and written language

M. A. K. Halliday

Series Editor: Frances Christie

Oxford University Press

Oxford University Press
Walton Street, Oxford OX2 6DP

Oxford   New York   Toronto
Delhi   Bombay   Calcutta   Madras   Karachi
Petaling Jaya   Singapore   Hong Kong   Tokyo
Nairobi   Dar es Salaam   Cape Town
Melbourne   Auckland

and associated companies in
Berlin   Ibadan

Oxford, *Oxford English* and the *Oxford English* logo are trade marks of
Oxford University Press

ISBN 019 437153 0

© Deakin University 1985, 1989

First published 1985
Second edition 1989
Second impression 1990

Printed in Hong Kong

About the author

M. A. K. Halliday

Michael Halliday was born in Leeds, England, in 1925. He took his BA at London University in Chinese language and literature, then studied linguistics as a graduate student, first in China (Peking University and Lingnan University, Canton) and then at Cambridge, where he received his PhD in 1955.

After holding appointments at Cambridge and Edinburgh he went to University College London in 1963, as Director of the Communication Research Centre. There he directed two research projects, one in the Linguistic Properties of Scientific English and the other in Linguistics and English Teaching; the latter produced *Breakthrough to Literacy* for lower primary schools and *Language in Use* for secondary schools. In 1965 he was appointed concurrently Professor of General Linguistics, with responsibility for building up a new department in this subject. He remained at University College London until the end of 1970. From 1973 to 1975 he was Professor of Linguistics at the University of Illinois, Chicago Circle. At the beginning of 1976 he became Head of the new Department of Linguistics at the University of Sydney, from which he recently retired. He was consultant to the Curriculum Development Centre's Language Development Project 1976–78 and subsequently a member of the Project Review and Advisory Panel.

He taught on the Linguistic Society of America's summer Linguistic Institutes in 1964 (Indiana), 1966 (UCLA), and 1973 (Michigan), and was elected to honorary membership of the Society in 1978. He has held visiting professorships at Yale, Brown, UC. Irvine, and the University of Nairobi; and in 1972-73 was a Fellow of the Centre for Advanced Study in the Behavioral Sciences at Stanford, California. In 1969 he was awarded an honorary doctorate at the University of Nancy, France; and in 1981 he received the David H.Russell Award for Distinguished Research in the Teaching of English from the National Council of Teachers of English (USA).

His current research interests are the semantics and grammar of

iii

modern English; language development in early childhood; text linguistics and register variation; educational applications of linguistics; and artificial intelligence, in which he is associated with the 'Penman' project at the Information Sciences Institute, University of Southern California.

Among his publications are:

The Language of the Chinese 'Secret History of the Mongols', Publications of the Philological Society, Vol. 17 (Blackwell, Oxford, 1959).

(With Angus McIntosh & Peter Strevens) *The Linguistic Sciences and Language Teaching* (Longman, London, 1964).

Intonation and Grammar in British English (Mouton, The Hague, 1967).

'Notes on transitivity and theme in English—Parts 1-3', *Journal of Linguistics*, vol. 3, 1967 and vol. 4, 1968.

A Course in Spoken English: Intonation (Oxford University Press, London, 1970).

Explorations in the Functions of Language (Edward Arnold, London, 1973).

Learning How to Mean: Explorations in the Development of Language (Edward Arnold, London, 1975).

(With Ruqaiya Hasan) *Cohesion in English* (Longman, London, 1976).

System and Function in Language, edited by Gunther Kress (Oxford University Press, London, 1976).

Language as Social Semiotic: The Social Interpretation of Language and Meaning (Edward Arnold, London, 1978).

(With J. R. Martin) (eds.) *Readings in Systemic Linguistics* (Batsford, London, 1981).

An Introduction to Functional Grammar (Edward Arnold, London, 1985).

Foreword

In a sense, educational interest in language is not new. Studies of rhetoric and of grammar go back as far as the Greeks; in the English-speaking countries, studies of the classical languages, and more recently of English itself, have had a well established place in educational practice. Moreover, a number of the issues which have aroused the most passionate debates about how to develop language abilities have tended to remain, resurfacing at various points in history in somewhat different formulations perhaps, but nonetheless still there, and still lively.

Of these issues, probably the most lively has been that concerning the extent to which explicit knowledge about language on the part of the learner is a desirable or a useful thing. But the manner in which discussion about this issue has been conducted has often been allowed to obscure other and bigger questions: questions, for example, both about the nature of language as an aspect of human experience, and about language as a resource of fundamental importance in the building of human experience. The tendency in much of the western intellectual tradition has been to dissociate language and experience, in such a way that language is seen as rather neutral, merely serving to 'carry' the fruits of experience. Whereas in this view language is seen as a kind of 'conduit', subservient to experience in various ways, an alternative view, as propounded in the books in this series, would argue that language is itself not only a part of experience, but intimately involved in the manner in which we construct and organise experience. As such, it is never neutral, but deeply implicated in building meaning. One's notions concerning how to teach about language will differ quite markedly, depending upon the view one adopts concerning language and experience. In fact, though discussions concerning teaching about language can sometimes be interesting, in practice many such discussions have proved theoretically ill-founded and barren, serving merely to perpetuate a number of unhelpful myths about language.

The most serious and confusing of these myths are those which would suggest we can dissociate language from meaning — form from function, or form from 'content'. Where such myths apply, teaching about language becomes a matter of teaching about 'language rules' — normally grammatical rules — and as history has demonstrated over the years, such teaching rapidly degenerates into the arid pursuit of parts of speech and the parsing of isolated sentences. Meaning, and the critical role of language in the building of meaning, are simply overlooked, and the kinds of knowledge about language made available to the learner are of a very limited kind.

The volumes in this series of monographs devoted to language education in my view provide a much better basis upon which to address questions related to the teaching about language than has been the case anywhere in the English-speaking world for some time now. I make this claim for several reasons, one of the most important being that the series never sought directly to establish a model for teaching about language at all. On the contrary, it sought to establish a principled model of language, which, once properly articulated, allows us to address many questions of an educational nature, including those to do with teaching about language. To use Halliday's term (1978), such a model sees language primarily as a 'social semiotic', and as a resource for meaning, centrally involved in the processes by which human beings negotiate, construct and change the nature of social experience. While the series certainly does not claim to have had the last word on these and related subjects, I believe it does do much to set a new educational agenda — one which enables us to look closely at the role of language both in living and in learning: one which, moreover, provides a basis upon which to decide those kinds of teaching and learning about language which may make a legitimate contribution to the development of the learner.

I have said that arguments to do with teaching about language have been around for a long time: certainly as long as the two hundred years of white settlement in Australia. In fact, coincidentally, just as the first settlers were taking up their enforced residence in the Australian colony of New South Wales, Lindley Murray was preparing his *English Grammar* (1795), which, though not the only volume produced on the subject in the eighteenth century, was certainly the best. Hundreds of school grammars that were to appear in Britain and Australia for the next century at least, were to draw very heavily upon what Murray had written. The parts of speech, parsing and sentence analysis, the latter as propounded by Morell (an influential inspector of schools in England), were the principal elements in the teaching about language in the Australian colonies, much as they were in England throughout the century. By the 1860s and 1870s the Professor of Classics and Logic at Sydney University, Charles Badham, who had arrived from England in 1867, publicly disagreed with the examining authorities in New South Wales concerning the teaching of grammar. To the contemporary reader there is a surprising modernity about many of his objections, most notably his strongly held conviction that successful control of one's language is learned less as a matter of committing to memory the parts of speech and the principles of parsing, than as a matter of frequent opportunity for use.

Historically, the study by which issues of use had been most effectively addressed had been that of rhetoric, in itself quite old in the English-speaking tradition, dating back at least to the sixteenth century. Rhetorical studies flourished in the eighteenth century, the best known works on the subject being George Campbell's *The Philosophy of Rhetoric* (1776), and Hugh Blair's *Lectures on Rhetoric and Belles Lettres* (1783), while in the nineteenth century Richard Whately published his work, *Elements of Rhetoric* (1828). As the nineteenth century proceeded, scholarly work on rhetoric declined, as was testified by the markedly inferior but nonetheless influential works of Alexander Bain (*English Composition and Rhetoric*, 1866; Revised version, 1887). Bain, in fact, did much to corrupt and destroy the older rhetorical traditions, primarily because he lost sight of the need for a basic concern with meaning in language. Bain's was the century of romanticism after all: on the one hand, Matthew Arnold was extolling the civilising influence of English literature in the development of children; on the other hand, there was a tendency towards suspicion, even contempt, for those who wanted to take a scholarly look at the linguistic organisation of texts, and at the ways in which they were structured for the building of meaning. In 1921, Ballard (who was an expert witness before the Newbolt Enquiry on the teaching of English), wrote a book called *Teaching the Mother Tongue*, in which he noted among other things, that unfortunately in England at least rhetorical studies had become associated with what were thought to be rather shallow devices for persuasion and argument. The disinclination to take seriously the study of the rhetorical organisation of texts gave rise to a surprisingly unhelpful tradition for the teaching of literature, which is with us yet in many places: 'civilising' it might be, but it was *not* to be the object of systematic study, for such study would in some ill-defined way threaten or devalue the work of literature itself.

A grammarian like Murray had never been in doubt about the relationship of grammar and rhetoric. As he examined it, grammar was concerned with the syntax of the written English sentence: it was not concerned with the study of 'style', about which he wrote a short appendix in his original grammar, where his debt to the major rhetoricians of the period was apparent. Rhetorical studies, especially as discussed by Campbell for instance, did address questions of 'style', always from the standpoint of a recognition of the close relationship of language to the socially created purpose in using language. In fact, the general model of language as discussed by Campbell bore some relationship to the model taken up in this series, most notably in its commitment to register.

The notion of register proposes a very intimate relationship of text to context: indeed, so intimate is that relationship, it is asserted, that the one can only be interpreted by reference to the other. Meaning is realised in language (in the form of text), which is thus shaped or patterned in response to the context of situation in which it is used. To study language then, is to concentrate upon exploring how it is systematically patterned towards important social ends. The linguistic theory adopted here is that of systemic linguistics. Such a linguistic theory is itself also a social theory, for it proposes firstly, that it is in the nature of human behaviour to build reality and/or experience through complex semiotic processes, and secondly, that the principal semiotic system available to humans is their language. In this sense, to study language is to explore some of the most important and pervasive of the processes by which human beings build their world.

I originally developed the volumes in this series as the basis of two major off campus courses in Language Education taught in the Master's degree program at Deakin University, Victoria, Australia. To the best of my knowledge, such courses, which are designed primarily for teachers and teacher educators, are the first of their kind in the world, and while they actually appeared in the mid 1980s, they emerge from work in language education which has been going on in Australia for some time. This included the national Language Development Project, to which Michael Halliday was consultant, and whose work I co-ordinated throughout its second, productive phase. (This major project was initiated by the Commonwealth Government's Curriculum Development Centre, Canberra, in the 1970s, and involved the co-operation of curriculum development teams from all Australian states in developing language curriculum materials. Its work was not completed because of political changes which caused the activities of the Curriculum Development Centre to be wound down.) In the 1980s a number of conferences have been held fairly regularly in different parts of Australia, all of them variously exploring aspects of language education, and leading to the publication of a number of conference reports. They include: Frances Christie (ed.), *Language and the Social Construction of Experience* (Deakin University, 1983); Brendan Bartlett and John Carr (eds.), *Language in Education Workshop: a Report of Proceedings* (Centre for Research and Learning, Brisbane C.A.E., Mount Gravatt Campus, Brisbane, 1984); Ruqaiya Hasan (ed.), *Discourse on Discourse* (Applied Linguistics Association of Australia, Occasional Papers, Number 7, 1985); Clare Painter and J.R. Martin (eds.), *Writing to Mean: Teaching Genres across the Curriculum* (Applied Linguistics Association of Australia, Occasional Papers, Number 9, 1986); Linda Gerot, Jane Oldenburg and Theo Van Leeuwen (eds.), *Language and Socialisation: Home and School* (in preparation). All these activities have contributed to the building of a climate of opinion and a tradition of thinking about language which made possible the development of the volumes in this series.

While it is true that the developing tradition of language education which these volumes represent does, as I have noted, take up some of the concerns of the older rhetorical studies, it nonetheless also looks forward, pointing to ways of examining language which were not available in earlier times. For example, the notion of language as a social semiotic, and its associated conception of experience or reality as socially built and constantly subject to processes of transformation, finds very much better expression today than would have been possible before, though obviously much more requires to be said about this than can be dealt with in these volumes. In addition, a functionally driven view of language is now available, currently most completely articulated in Halliday's *An Introduction to Functional Grammar* (1985), which offers ways of understanding the English language in a manner that Murray's Grammar could not have done.

Murray's Grammar confined itself to considerations of the syntax of the written English sentence. It did not have anything of use to say about spoken language, as opposed to written language, and, equally, it provided no basis upon which to explore a unit other than the sentence, whether that be the paragraph, or, even more importantly, the total text. The preoccupation with the written sentence neglected the pre-eminent position being accorded to the written word by Murray's time, leading to disastrous consequences since, because of the diminished value accorded to spoken language, especially in educational practices. In Murray's work, the lack of a direct relationship between the study of grammar on the one hand, and that of 'style', on the other hand, was, as I have already noted, to be attributed to his view that it was the rhetorician who addressed wider questions relating to the text. In the tradition in which he worked, in fact, grammar looked at syntactic rules divorced from considerations of meaning or social purpose.

By contrast, Halliday's approach to grammar has a number of real strengths, the first of which is the fact that its basis is semantic, not syntactic: that is to say, it is a semantically driven grammar, which, while not denying that certain principles of syntax do apply, seeks to consider and identify the role of various linguistic items in any text in terms of their function in building meaning. It is for this reason that its practices for interpreting and labelling various linguistic items and groupings are functionally based, not syntactically based. There is in other words, no dissociation of 'grammar' on the one hand and 'semantics' or meaning on the other. A second strength of Halliday's approach is that it is not uniquely interested in written language, being instead committed to the study of both the spoken and written modes, and to an explanation of the differences between the two, in such a way that each is illuminated because of its contrast with the other. A third and final strength of the systemic functional grammar is that it permits useful movement across the text, addressing the manner in which linguistic patternings are built up for the construction of the overall text in its particular 'genre', shaped as it is in response to the context of situation which gave rise to it.

Halliday's functional grammar lies behind all ten volumes in this series, though one other volume, by Michael Christie, called *Aboriginal perspectives on experience and learning: the role of language in Aboriginal Education*, draws upon somewhat different if still compatible perspectives in educational and language theory to develop its arguments. The latter volume, is available directly from Deakin University. In varying ways, the volumes in this series provide a helpful introduction to much that is more fully dealt with in Halliday's Grammar, and I commend the series to the reader who wants to develop some sense of the ways such a body of linguistic theory can be applied to educational questions. A version of the grammar specifically designed for teacher education remains to be written, and while I cherish ambitions to begin work on such a version soon, I am aware that others have similar ambitions − in itself a most desirable development.

While I have just suggested that the reader who picks up any of the volumes in this series should find ways to apply systemic linguistic theory to educational theory, I want to argue, however, that what is offered here is more than merely a course in applied linguistics, legitimate though such a course might be. Rather, I want to claim that this is a course in educational linguistics, a term of importance because it places linguistic study firmly at the heart of educational enquiry. While it is true that a great deal of linguistic research of the past, where it did not interpret language in terms of interactive, social processes, or where it was not grounded in a concern for meaning, has had little of relevance to offer education, socially relevant traditions of linguistics like that from which systemics is derived, do have a lot to contribute. How that contribution should be articulated is quite properly a matter of development in partnership between educationists, teachers and linguists, and a great deal has yet to be done to achieve such articulation.

I believe that work in Australia currently is making a major contribution to the development of a vigorous educational linguistics, not all of it of course in a systemic framework. I would note here the important work of such people as J.R. Martin, Joan Rothery, Suzanne Eggins and Peter Wignell of the University of Sydney, investigating children's writing development; the innovatory work of Brian Gray and his colleagues a few years ago in developing language programs for Aboriginal children in central Australia, and more recently his work with other groups in Canberra; the recent work of Beth Graham, Michael Christie and Stephen Harris, all of the Northern Territory Department of Education, in developing language programs for Aboriginal children; the important work of John Carr and his colleagues of the Queensland Department of Education in developing new perspectives upon language in the various language curriculum guidelines they have prepared for their state; the contributions of Jenny Hammond of the University of Wollongong, New South Wales, in her research into language development in schools, as well as the various programs in which she teaches; research being undertaken by Ruqaiya Hasan and Carmel Cloran of Macquarie University, Sydney, into children's language learning styles in the transition years from home to school; investigations by Linda Gerot, also of Macquarie University, into classroom discourse in the secondary school, across a number of different subjects; and the work of Pam Gilbert of James Cook University, Townsville, in Queensland, whose interests are both in writing in the secondary school, and in language and gender.

The signs are that a coherent educational linguistics is beginning to appear around the world, and I note with pleasure the appearance of two new and valuable international journals: *Language and Education*, edited by David Corson of Massey University, New Zealand, and *Linguistics in Education*, edited by David Bloome, of the University of Massachusetts. Both are committed to the development of an educational linguistics, to which many traditions of study, linguistic, semiotic and sociological, will no doubt make an important contribution. Such an educational linguistics is long overdue, and in what are politically difficult times, I suggest such a study can make a major contribution to the pursuit of educational equality of opportunity, and to attacking the wider social problems of equity and justice. Language is a political institution: those who are wise in its ways, capable of using it to shape and serve important personal and social goals, will be the ones who are 'empowered' (to use a fashionable word): able, that is, not merely to participate effectively *in* the world, but able also *to act upon it*, in the sense that they can strive for significant social change. Looked at in these terms, provision of appropriate language education programs is a profoundly important matter, both in ensuring equality of educational opportunity, and in helping to develop those who are able and willing to take an effective role in democratic processes of all kinds.

One of the most encouraging measures of the potential value of the perspectives open to teachers taking up an educational linguistics of the kind offered in these monographs, has been the variety of teachers attracted to the courses of which they form a part, and the ways in which these teachers have used what they have learned in undertaking research papers for the award of the master's degree. They include, for example, secondary teachers of physics, social science, geography and English, specialists in teaching English as a second language to migrants and specialists in teaching English to Aboriginal people, primary school teachers, a nurse educator, teachers of illiterate adults, and language curriculum consultants, as well as a number of teacher educators with specialist responsibilities in teaching language education. For many of these people the perspectives offered by an educational linguistics are both new and challenging, causing them to review and change aspects of their teaching practices in various ways. Coming to terms with a semantically driven grammar is in itself quite demanding, while there is often considerable effort involved to bring to conscious awareness the ways in which we use language for the realisation of different meanings. But the effort is plainly worth it, principally because of the added sense of control and direction it can give teachers interested to work at fostering and developing students who are independent and confident in using language for the achievement of various goals. Those people for whom these books have proved helpful, tend to say that they have achieved a stronger and richer appreciation of language and how it works than they had before; that because they know considerably more about language themselves, they are able to intervene much more effectively in directing and guiding those whom they teach; that because they have a better sense of the relationship of language and 'content' than they had before, they can better guide their students into control of the 'content' of the various subjects for which they are responsible; and finally, that because they have an improved sense of how to direct language learning, they are able to institute new assessment policies, negotiating, defining and clarifying realistic goals for their students. By any standards, these are considerable achievements.

As I draw this Foreword to a close, I should perhaps note for the reader's benefit the manner in which students doing course work with me are asked to read the monographs in this series, though I should stress that the books were deliberately designed to be picked up and read in any order one likes. In the first of the two semester courses, called *Language and Learning*, students are asked to read the following volumes in the order given:

Frances Christie — *Language education*
Clare Painter — *Learning the mother tongue*
M.A.K. Halliday & Ruqaiya Hasan — *Language, context, and text: aspects of language in a social-semiotic perspective*
J.L. Lemke — *Using language in the classroom*
then either,
M.A.K. Halliday — *Spoken and written language*
or,
Ruqaiya Hasan — *Linguistics, language, and verbal art.*

The following four volumes, together with the one by Michael Christie, mentioned above, belong to the second course called *Sociocultural Aspects of Language and Education*, and they may be read by the students in any order they like, though only three of the five need be selected for close study:

David Butt — *Talking and thinking: the patterns of behaviour*
Gunther Kress — *Linguistic processes in sociocultural practice*
J.R. Martin — *Factual writing: exploring and challenging social reality*
Cate Poynton — *Language and gender: making the difference*

References

Bain, A., *An English Grammar* (Longman, Roberts and Green, London, 1863).

Bain, A., *English Composition and Rhetoric*, revised in two Parts — *Part 1, Intellectual Elements of Style*, and *Part 11, Emotional Qualities of Style* (Longman, Green and Company, London, 1887).

Ballard, P., *Teaching the Mother Tongue* (Hodder & Stoughton, London, 1921).

Blair, H., *Lectures on Rhetoric and Belles Lettres, Vols. 1 and 11* (W. Strahan and T. Cadell, London, 1783).

Campbell, G., (new ed.), *The Philosophy of Rhetoric* (T. Tegg and Son, London, 1838). Originally published (1776).

Halliday, M.A.K., *Language as social semiotic: the social interpretation of language and meaning* (Edward Arnold, London, 1978).

Halliday, M.A.K., *An Introduction to Functional Grammar* (Edward Arnold, London, 1985).

Murray, Lindley, *English Grammar* (1795), Facsimile Reprint No. 106 (Menston, Scolar Press, 1968).

Contents

Preface

We live in what is called a 'literate society', which means that a reasonably large proportion of older children and adults in the community use language in a written as well as in a spoken form. They have learnt to read and write. Speaking and listening come naturally, unless one is born deaf; they also have to be learnt, of course, but—like walking and running—they are learnt young and without benefit of instruction. To get to read and write, however, one is usually taught; this is one step, perhaps the most important step, in the process of education. Reading and writing are associated with educated practice from the start.

Writing and speaking are not just alternative ways of doing the same things; rather, they are ways of doing different things. Writing evolves when language has to take on new functions in society. These tend to be the prestigious functions, those associated with learning, religion, government, and trade.

Partly because of its association with the sources of authority and power—but partly also because it is nearer the surface of our consciousness—writing tends to steal the linguistic limelight. For most literate people, 'language' means written language. We talk about how letters are pronounced, instead of, more accurately, how sounds are written down. We say our language is 'not phonetic', meaning that the spoken forms do not accord with the writing system—whereas in fact it is the written forms that do not accord with the sound system. Even the notion of a 'word' is tied to the written mode. And if something is written down, we are much more likely to believe it. It is no wonder that, as teachers, we tend to assume that written language is the only respectable medium through which to learn.

But speech came first, by some millions of years; and it comes first in our life history as individuals. We may have learnt to read and write, but we still go on talking and listening; and we still go on learning by talking and listening. The fact that we are less conscious of the processes of speech does not make them any the less important. We achieve different goals by means of spoken and written language; but neither has any superior value over the other.

Much of the time, of course, we are doing a bit of both, without any very clear boundary between them. And I would like you to approach this book rather in that spirit. It had to be written, because Deakin University wanted it in book form and not on tape; also it contains a lot of figures and diagrams, as well as tables that may need to be consulted over and over again, which is one of the things that writing is particularly good for. But I was saying it to myself all the time as I wrote it; and if there are any passages in it that seem to be difficult, I recommend reading them aloud. Readers read differently, of course, just as writers write differently; but I think that for some people, at least, the meaning will stand out more clearly once the text is 'heard' in spoken form.

I would like to thank Mr Ding Zhaozhang for his kindness in writing the Chinese characters for me; his calligraphic skill is greatly appreciated. I am extremely grateful to Deakin University for the trouble they have taken, and to the Series Editor, Frances Christie for her patient prodding and constructive advice. It is fashionable these days to talk about 'intertextuality'; this text is to be thought of as in dialogue with the other texts in the series, the whole lot together trying to say something about language as the basis of human development.

M. A. K. Halliday

Chapter 1
Development of speech

Origins

It seems likely that human beings have been around in the world for quite some time: say 2−3 million years, according to the findings of Richard Leakey and others. If we met one of our ancestors of that antiquity, we would recognise him or her as quite like one of ourselves.

The distinctively human characteristics of walking upright, using tools, and talking were already appearing well over a million years ago. These are supposed to mark us off from the rest of creation, including our immediate forebears. It is customary nowadays to emphasise the continuity—that which we share with other species—rather than the discontinuity; and to interpret what distinguishes us against the background of what we have in common—with the apes, and with our more distant but also highly intelligent cousins the dolphins. So let us look at language in this light.

What is it that distinguishes human language from communication in other species? There have been many attempts to demonstrate that apes could acquire human-like language; that although their articulatory organs are not shaped to produce speech sounds, if we free them from the constraints of articulation and allow them to use some other form of output, like pressing particular keys in particular sequences, it can be shown that they would be intellectually capable of learning our kind of language.

The results are impressive, although they turn out on examination to be not as startling as was initially claimed. The idea that 'they could talk if they wanted; they just don't need to' is somewhat naïve, based on an oversimplified account of what human language is really like. (It also seems rather unlikely, one must admit.) So let us speculate about how, on the basis of our present knowledge, human language probably evolved; and see at what point and in what respects our ancestors set out along a new semiotic track.

The developmental analogy

programme
'Lifelines: exploring
the development of
human talents'

It is often pointed out that in many respects the individual recapitulates the history of the species. The idea is an old one, first formulated as an explicit principle by Ernst Häckel. In the words of a recent BBC television series, 'as an embryo growing in the womb, each one of us takes the form of fish, then amphibian and mammal, and finally prepares for life as a member of much the most varied and flexible species to have evolved on earth'.

The evolutionary process does not stop at birth; but it changes direction, because the born child is a social being and will therefore develop social characteristics alongside the purely biological ones. As he learns to walk, he also learns to talk. (It is quite likely that he has learnt something of his mother tongue even before he is born; the rhythm of speech begins in the diaphragm, and the child must feel the regular variation in pressure that is produced by the muscles controlling the outflow of air as his mother talks. If so, he may already be predisposed at birth to the rhythmic patterns of his 'mother tongue', in the strict sense of the term: the language that is spoken by his mother.)

Brazelton

The individual
develops the way the
species evolved.

If the notion that ontogeny recapitulates phylogeny is in general valid as a principle of biological development, we may also find it to be valid for certain aspects of social development—at least for one particular aspect, that of the learning of language. There is a caution to be given here, however. Where biological development is concerned, the evolution of the species is established on other grounds; the evidence is independent of any developmental findings and hence if we find the individual retracing the history of the species we are discovering something new.

In the case of language, however, we cannot reconstruct the early stages of its evolution. Almost the only evidence we have for this is derived from what we know about how children learn language. The independent information is simply the probability that early humans in this period did have language, as is suggested (1) by the size of their brains and (2) by the fact that they used tools. But these tell us nothing about what kind of a language they had or how it evolved. For this we have to guess from studying the development of the child.

Does child language
then trace the path
of linguistic
evolution?

Such guesses are just that—guesswork. On the other hand, there are some striking features about language development in early childhood that suggest that here too the parallel may be fairly close: in particular, the fact of the PROTOLANGUAGE—that children typically start by creating language for themselves before moving over to the language they hear around them. Before the mother tongue there is a 'child tongue', and the forms and functions that that takes look very much like evolutionary steps towards what we know as language today.

Symbolic and non-symbolic acts

Children begin to communicate more or less from birth. A newborn child can already 'pay attention': when his mother talks to him, he listens. Within three or four weeks he is contributing his own share of

2

the 'discussion', responding with animated movements of his body—his arms and legs, and also his tongue and his lips.

This bodily activity is not yet language. Colwyn Trevarthen (1978, 1979), who was one of the first to study these processes, calls the tongue and lip movements 'pre-speech', because the baby seems to be rehearsing the muscular activity that will be used to produce speech later on; just as with his arms he performs a sequence of reaching out, grasping, and pulling towards him that is like taking hold of an object—'pre-reaching', in Trevarthen's terms. He is preparing himself, so to speak, for the two basic skills he will first have to master—using tools, and talking. In the first, he will be using his limbs, and extensions of his limbs, to control his environment directly, and to orient and manoeuvre himself within it. With the second, speech, he will be using other muscular movements and postures, those of articulation—also to control his environment; but in this case to control it indirectly, by acting on others so that they will control it for him. For this he has to learn to act symbolically.

Let us make this distinction clear, the distinction between symbolic and non-symbolic acts. If I am hungry, and want to eat an apple, I can act directly on the apple by going and getting it myself—moving to where it is in reach, reaching out, and then grabbing it. But—provided there are other human beings around—I can get hold of it in another way, by acting not directly but symbolically. I can say to a sympathetic member of my family 'Fetch me an apple'.

non-symbolic and symbolic action: the origin of 'acts of meaning'

This is a symbolic act, an ACT OF MEANING. It has to be addressed to someone—not necessarily some particular person, maybe just to the world at large; but unless there is a receiver it will not work. Acts of meaning are by their nature social acts, and all symbolic systems are social systems. Of course, once a system of symbols has come into being, it can be played with, fought with, turned into an art form; it can be used to address oneself, a deity, or even animals or inanimate objects. But these are secondary, derivative uses; the symbols could never have evolved to serve these functions, because they depend on values the symbols have already acquired in use.

All symbols are social.

Somewhere around the middle of the first year of life, the child lays the foundations for these two modes of action, the direct and the symbolic. He learns to reach out, grasp, and pull things towards him, and he learns the complementary action of hitting things to knock them away: 'I want', 'I don't want'. This, typically, starts around 4–5 months. Not long afterwards, he begins to explore the alternative, symbolic mode—getting others to achieve the effect for him.

The 'child tongue'

But there is a problem with symbolic acts. A symbol has to be understood. If I start speaking Chinese to you, that is a perfectly good act of meaning; but if you do not understand Chinese, the only message you will get is that I am talking—you will have no idea what I am talking about. Even if what I am saying is the Chinese equivalent of 'bring me an apple' (ná pínguǒ lái gěi wǒ), it is unlikely that the apple will arrive.

So how does a human infant go about creating a set of symbols, such that those around him will understand? It used to be assumed that he went straight into the mother tongue, copying the words as well as he could and eventually learning to combine them. Later on, in his second year, that is what he does; but a great deal has already happened before he starts on the mother tongue. Before he takes over the language of others, he starts by creating one for himself—by himself in interaction with the small group of others who learn it along with him.

Before the mother
tongue comes a
'child tongue',
referred to as 'proto-
language'.

At 7−8 months, he is ready to act symbolically. But he cannot start straightaway on the mother tongue: not only because he could not yet control its **sounds**, though this is true too, but more importantly because he could not yet control its **forms** and its **meanings**. Adult languages are organised around a grammar (more accurately, a LEXICO-GRAMMAR, a code consisting of words-in-structure), which has the function of translating the meanings into the sounds; but an eight-month-old can have no idea of what a word is, since it is something that involves a particular kind of abstraction. So he has to create a symbolic system of his own, one that does not contain either vocabulary or grammar but consists of a little set of SIGNS. These signs are made by voice, or gesture, or some combination of the two.

There have been very few studies of the first step, the initial symbolic acts of meaning by which an infant starts to 'mean'; so it is impossible to give a general account of how this happens. Instead, I will tell the story as it happened with one particular child—a boy whose name, for present purposes, is Nigel. Here is a brief account of how Nigel created his first language.

How Nigel started to mean

One day at eight months old, Nigel was sitting on his mother's knee. She was writing. As she paused, with the pen held lightly in her fingers, Nigel reached out for it. He closed his fist firmly around it, looked at her face for a moment, and then, after another moment, let go. He had not tried to pull it towards him.

His mother said 'You want the pen, do you? All right—you can hold it, for a little while'.

This was an act of meaning; and it had worked. His mother had understood. Nigel was, of course, quite capable of grabbing the pen and pulling it towards him; that was his normal way of getting something. But on this occasion, he had not taken it; he had asked for it. He had created a symbol, by the use of his hand—it was gestural, not vocal; and he had waited for the response. There was a clear distinction between the two kinds of act: the direct, non-symbolic action on the object itself, and the indirect, symbolic action 'on' (i.e. directed towards) the object but 'through' (mediated by) the person addressed.

how to create a
symbol that others
understand: the
iconic principle

Nigel had solved the basic problem, that of creating a symbol that could be understood; and he had solved it iconically—that is, by creating a symbol that bore a natural resemblance to its meaning. The gesture of grasping an object firmly and holding on to it for a measurable time before letting go is a very reasonable way of encoding the meaning

'I want that thing', 'let me hold it', 'give it to me'. And his mother's response showed him she had understood. (She had acted entirely spontaneously, not at all becoming conscious of the fact that both Nigel and she had performed something entirely new.)

Nigel was encouraged by his success and created two more symbols within the same week, both of them also iconic. I was entertaining him by throwing his toy cat up in the air, and catching it as it came down. When I stopped, he leant forward and touched it: neither grasping it nor pushing it away, but keeping his fingers pressed against it for a measurable time.

'You want me to throw it up again?' Every time I stopped, he repeated the gesture, until I got tired and refused. But it was clear that I had got the message; and Nigel himself made it clear, by the satisfaction he showed at being understood.

A day or two later, his mother offered him his woolly dog to play with. He touched it with just one finger, very lightly and for the briefest instant, then took his hand away. She offered it to him again; he repeated the gesture. It meant 'No, I don't want it; take it away'. She understood, said 'Don't you want it?', and put it down. Again, it was a symbolic gesture; he could push objects away if he didn't want them, but this was quite distinct. He was 'saying' 'I don't want it', and his mother was responding to the symbol.

These were not, in fact, the very first symbols Nigel had created; these had appeared two weeks earlier, at shortly before the age of eight months. They were vocal, not gestural; and each consisted of a single vowel, the same vowel [œ] (like the French word œufs) but with a slight difference in tone. One, on a low, breathy tone, meant 'yes it's me, and here we are together'.

verbal and gestural symbols; a child's first meaning

His mother came to him. 'Hello, bootie', she said.
'œ', he replied.
'There's my bootie!'
'œ'.
'That's nice, yes.'
'œ'.

This would go on for as long as she kept the conversation going.

The other was also [œ], but on a higher, falling tone, and without the breathy, sighing quality of the first. It meant 'That's interesting— what's happening?', and was used when Nigel's attention was caught by some commotion, like a flock of birds taking off from the ground or a bus revving up its engine. This was addressed mainly to himself; but often someone responded, saying what the commotion was all about.

'Those are pigeons', his mother said. 'Weren't they noisy?'

One child's protolanguage

So at eight months Nigel had a language. It consisted of five signs, which were frequently repeated when the occasion arose; and those around him, the small group that made up his immediate family, understood them and gave a reply. They replied, of course, in their own language, not in his; Nigel would no doubt have been insulted to have his own signs served back to him, but it never occurred to anyone to try. What mattered was that he could now converse: he could initiate a conversation and be understood. From that moment, his route into language was open.

For its relevance to linguistic evolution, we need to interpret this little system, and then to follow Nigel through one stage further.

The ability to mean is important to Nigel because it is functional. He is creating a language for a purpose, to do something with it. If we watch him at eight months and notice the environments in which he is using these signs (the CONTEXT OF SITUATION, in linguistic terminology), we will be aware of two kinds of motive that lead him to communicate. One is a pragmatic one: he wants to be given something, or he wants something to be done for him; and for these purposes he used the iconic gestures of grasping and touching. The other is a more thoughtful mode; either he is expressing curiosity about what is going on around him, or he is just 'being together', expressing his awareness that he is one person, his mother is another, and that they are sharing an experience. These he expresses by sound, his first true speech sounds.

motives for communicating in the first year of life

Having established his ability to mean, and gained recognition as a conversation partner, at 9½–10 months, he set about creating a rich protolanguage that would serve him until he was ready to start on English. At 10½ months, he had a range of twelve distinct signs; by 12 months, this had increased to 20; by 13½ months, to 27; by 15 months, to 31; and by 16½ months, to 50. By this time, however, he is beginning the transition into the mother tongue and his language is no longer of the strictly 'proto' kind.

If we look at the period of roughly six months that constitutes, with Nigel, the period of the true protolanguage—say 9½–15½ months of age—we find a very clear pattern of functional development, which we can interpret in terms of these same two motifs. Let us exemplify from right in the middle of this six-month period, when Nigel is just over one year of age and just about beginning to walk. On the one hand, he has a range of pragmatic signs including the following:

'give me that'	na . . .	(mid fall)
'yes I want that thing there'	yi . . .	(high level)
'yes I want what you just said'	a:	(high rise-fall)
'do that again'	ã	(mid fall)
'do that right now!'	m̄n̄ŋ	(high fall; loud)
'yes (let's) do that'	ã . . .	(low fall)
'no, don't (let's) do that'	ã.ã	(mid fall + mid fall)
'let's go out for a walk'		(slow glottal creak)

Note: . . . indicates that the sound was repeated, normally three or four times over.

On the other hand, he had a range of signs in the interactional and personal areas, including:

'hallo Anna!'	an:na	(high level + high level)
'yes it's me; I'm here'	ε:	(low fall, long drawn out)
'look, a picture; you say what it is'	a::da	(high rise + mid fall)
'nice to see you; let's look at this'	ededede	(proclitic + high level + high fall)

6

'I can hear an aeroplane'	œ.œ	(low fall + low fall)
'that's nice'	æyi:	(mid level + mid fall)
'that's funny (where's it gone?)'	m͡nŋ	(high rise-fall)
'a lot of talk!'	bwgabwga	(low fall + low fall)
'I'm sleepy'	gʷɣɪ . . .	(low level)

Apart from some instances of the last, which he also used in the special sense of playing a game of pretending to go to sleep, curling up on the floor in a little ball and closing his eyes tight, these all expressed some form of the relationship between himself and his environment: either interaction with another person, or pleasure, curiosity, disgust etc. in the outside world (or, in the last case, withdrawal from it). In one or two critical cases, the two components are combined: a fundamental theme in the protolanguage is that of 'let's look at this together', typically a greeting or calling to attention of the other person with an invitation to share an experience. It turns out that this sharing of experience by attending to some object that both can focus on— Nigel and his mother looking at a picture together, for example—is an important step towards the child's conception of a name, and hence towards the development of language in the adult sense.

learning to name things

What is the primary function of signs such as these? If those of the first group represent language in a 'doing' function—that which we refer to as PRAGMATIC—then the signs of the second group have more of a 'thinking' function: Nigel is using his ability to create meanings as a way of projecting himself on to the environment, expressing his concern with it—what's in it for him, so to speak—and so beginning systematically to explore it. In my own work I have referred to this as the MATHETIC function, meaning 'for learning with'.

Nigel's protolanguage, from its earliest origins, displays these two symbolic modes: to put it in other terms, it is at once both a means of action and a means of reflection. Parallel studies that have been carried out with other children suggest that this twofold functional orientation is a general feature of children's language construction; see, in particular, Clare Painter's book *Learning the Mother Tongue*. We shall not pursue the story further here. But it is important to point out, as we move away from the developmental perspective, that this complementarity of action and reflection persists way beyond the protolinguistic stage. In the first place, it serves as the central strategy by which children move out of their protolanguage and make the transition to the language (or languages) of their cultural environment. And finally, it is also the fundamental organising principle that lies behind the whole of adult language. Every human language is a potential for meaning in these two ways: it is a resource for doing with, and it is a resource for thinking with. This is the most important single fact about human language, and a motif to which we shall return in our study of speech and writing.

Painter (1989)

'pragmatic' and 'mathetic': language as a resource for doing and for learning

Evolutionary interpretations

Returning to Trevarthen for a moment: he made some films, in the early 1970s, showing mothers interacting with small infants, 8–10 weeks old.

7

The mother and child were facing each other; but Trevarthen had two cameras synchronised, and the picture was spliced so that each could be seen full face at the same time. The impression was striking: a kind of *pas de deux*, in which mother and baby, though performing what were obviously totally different movements, were yet in a curious way involved in a dance together, with remarkable synchrony. Then the film was shown in slow motion; and you could see that the child's movements were slightly ahead of the mother's. So although the child did not become animated until the mother's attention was directed to him— the initial invitation came from the mother—once the music started, so to speak, it was the child who was leading the dance.

This is the pattern of all subsequent language learning—except that, once he is mobile, the child does not wait to be invited; he can initiate the interaction. But the impetus always comes from the child; he is pushing forward the frontiers of language, with the mother, and others close enough to be in his little speech fellowship, tracking as he goes along. The others 'know' the language too—quite unconsciously; if you ask a mother who is conversing with a child at the protolinguistic stage what the child is saying, she will probably answer the way one such mother did to me, rather scornfully: 'He's not saying anything. He can't talk yet'—this at the end of an animated exchange between the two of them in which the child had been talking a large part of the time. It is a natural human tendency to want to mean.

It seems plausible—though it cannot be proved or disproved— that the child's way in to language is somehow analogous to the way language evolved in the human species. According to such an account, language would have begun in the form of a small number of signs for expressing general meanings relating to the needs of human beings in their relations with others: meanings such as 'give me (some object)', 'do (some service) for me', 'behave (in a certain way) for me', and also 'be together with me', 'come and look (at this) with me', 'I like (that)', 'I'm curious (about that)', 'I don't like (that)', and so on. The essential function of the symbol is that of sharing: shared action, or shared reflection.

how meanings may have evolved

Then (following the model of the child), particular (individual) persons and particular (classes of) objects come to be associated in regular, repetitive contexts with general meanings of this kind. So a particular sign evolves as 'I want to be together **with you**' and that becomes a name of a person or a kin relationship; another evolves as 'give me (a particular kind of) food', and so becomes the word for food, or some class of edible things; another as 'I'm curious about (the animal that's making) **that noise**', and so becomes the name of the animal species; and so on. The process by which a sign meaning some such unanalysed semantic complex turns into a name can be directly observed with a small child, so we know that it can happen; and the fact that this seems to be the **typical** developmental pattern suggests that the human experience may not have been very different.

Note that we are not here discussing the origin of the **form** of the expression: the phonetic or gestural shape of the protolinguistic sign. It is possible to say something about that too, from what can be observed of the way small children create the expressions for their protolanguage; the picture is far from clear, in any detail, at this stage, but the principle that the most effective symbol is one that is in some sense 'natural'—related iconically to its meaning—has presumably always held good.

1. We can see, for example, how children take the sounds they have heard themselves make naturally and turn them into protolinguistic signs: Nigel's long-drawn-out and breathy [ɛ̄ːː] 'yes it's me, I'm here' (subsequently 'yes that's what I meant', a signal that his meaning had been properly interpreted) originated as a sigh, a release of tension on being called by a voice he recognised; while his [gʲʷʏɪ] was a self-imitation of the sound he had heard himself make when going to sleep, thumb in front of lips and breath going in and out creating suction noises.
2. We can easily recognise 'other-imitations', the noise of ducks and cats and aeroplanes.
3. There is a tendency that is not well understood for small children's pragmatic signs to incorporate nasality; perhaps simply because it takes a positive muscular effort to close off the nasal passage.
4. Some prosodic and paralinguistic features seem naturally related to certain meanings: loudness with intensity of feeling, falling tone with definitiveness (certainty), rising tone with tentativeness (uncertainty), and so on.

how expressions may have evolved

All these factors may have played a part in the evolution of language; we cannot say. Languages change very quickly; they have had so many generations to evolve—say 50 000 generations at least—that there is no trace of their origin left in modern speech. (Onomatopoeic words are not relics from the remote past; they are remodelled every few generations.) It is perhaps useful to be reminded here that there is no such thing as a 'primitive' language: all languages in the world today are equally the product of this long process of evolution, and all are equally well adapted to the cultures whose needs they serve.

From protolanguage to language

In other words, all human languages are equally far removed from the 'protolanguage' stage we must have passed through in the early evolution of *homo loquens*. But as to exactly how the protolanguage may have evolved into a language of the type represented by all languages today, we can say very little—because here even the developmental evidence is lacking.

The reason for this is an interesting one. If we are right, then for the first 6−9 months after creating his first symbolic signs, a child is in some sense recapitulating the history of language. But then he takes a leap. There is, after all, no need for him to go through the whole process, step by laborious step; as soon as he is ready to take up the mother tongue, he can do so. He has in fact been listening to it for a long time; when he has reached the point where he can understand how grammar works—typically a few months into the second year—he can start building it up for himself. (Some children like to think about

the leap from child tongue to mother tongue

9

it for quite a long time before actually plunging in, and worry their parents by remaining quite uncommunicative till they are three years old; but provided they show understanding of what is said to them, the development is still taking place.)

Since there was no more advanced model around when our ancestors were evolving language, presumably they did not take any such leap—although we cannot be sure. There is a critical difference between a protolanguage and a language, a threshold that has to be crossed; there is no intermediate stage. (There can be a **mixture** between the two, and typically there is with children; the first features of 'language', in the adult sense, may appear quite early in the proto-linguistic phase, while equally, protolanguage features may continue well on into the development of language. Some are in fact still present in adult speech: so-called 'interjections' like *Ah!* and *Ow!* are in fact relics of protolanguage that have survived in adult speech.) So it may be that there is a leap at this point in evolution as well.

What is significant for our present discussion is not how the transition was made, but the nature of the transition itself. What is the essential difference between language and protolanguage?

important differences between language and protolanguage

Essentially, the difference is this. A language is a three-level ('tristratal') system. It consists of meanings, which are coded in wordings, which are then recoded in sounds. In technical linguistic terms, it consists of three levels, or 'strata': a SEMANTIC level, a GRAMMATICAL (strictly, 'lexico-grammatical') level, and a PHONOLOGICAL level. It does not code meaning directly into sound.

A protolanguage, on the other hand, is a two-level ('bistratal') system. It consists of meanings that are coded directly into sounds. Or rather, we should say into 'expressions', since as we have seen, the protolinguistic sign may be expressed either in sound or in gesture. (When language evolved, sound took over as the primary medium of expression—it has the obvious advantage that the receiver does not need to watch what the sender is doing, or even to be able to see the sender at all.) So let us say protolanguage consists simply of meanings and expressions.

As far as we know, all communication systems in species other than man are protolanguages. It may be that, as claimed in some of the studies referred to earlier, chimpanzees or gorillas are capable of operating with language; but this is doubtful—none of the examples given is conclusive in this respect, and it seems strange that if their brain is capable of doing so, they have not in fact begun to evolve any such system among themselves. Nearer home, we find protolanguage in our pets: cats and dogs communicate in this way, at least to us (apparently rather less among themselves). In all these species, the basic unit of communication is a protolinguistic sign: some unanalysed semantic bundle (for example, 'I'm hungry—feed me!') coded into some fixed expression (for example, a particular miaow, or a rubbing of the head against some object).

the limitations of the protolanguage: what it cannot do

A system of this kind is subject to various limitations, the principal one being that it is impossible to mean more than one thing at once. To do that, it is necessary to be able to take the elements of a message apart and recombine them in all sorts of different ways; but

10

the constituents of a two-level system are fixed and immutable, like a system of traffic signals—they have to be, otherwise the system would not work. They cannot be taken apart and recombined. (They can be strung out in a sequence, which gives an appearance of flexibility; but falsely, since the meaning of the sequence is simply the sum of its parts.) To be able to signal 'My friend here is hungry', or 'Are you hungry?', or even 'I'm not hungry', you have to have a three-level system, in which the various components of meaning can be teased apart, coded separately by different devices (selection, modification, ordering, prosodic modulation, etc.—all the paraphernalia of grammar and vocabulary, in fact), and then recoded into a single integrated output.

There comes a point, therefore, in the life of the individual, when the protolanguage can no longer serve his needs; and the same thing must have happened in the history of the race. It may be possible to **use** tools, with only a protolanguage; but it is certainly not possible to **make** them. To become toolmakers, we had to have language.

For a diagrammatic representation of the difference between language and protolanguage, see Figure 1.1.

Figure 1.1   Language and protolanguage

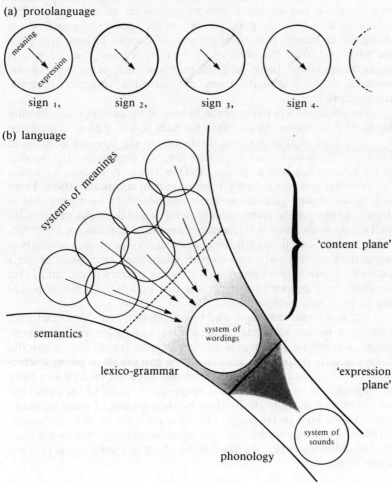

11

Chapter 2
Writing systems

Pictures and written symbols

The key to language, then, is grammar, the level of 'words-in-structure'; since that is where the meanings are organised, processed, and packaged in a form that can be turned into an expression of some kind. (That is looking at it from the point of view of the speaker, the one who is doing the encoding. It is equally valid, of course, to look at it from the other end, from the point of view of the listener, the one who is doing the decoding. In his case, the grammar takes in the expressions, unpacks them, and sorts them out into the different semantic components.)

For about 99.5 per cent of the history of the human race, the only medium of expression for language has been sound, the sound produced by the organs of speech (from the larynx to the lips and nostrils) in modifying the stream of air that comes from the diaphragm. The 'sender' of the message has been a speaker, and the 'receiver' has been a listener.

Not that this was the only form of human **communication**. From at least a thousand generations back, our ancestors have been able to draw, and have made pictures on rock faces and the walls of caves (as well as, no doubt, on much less durable material that has not survived). Whatever the specific significance and social value of such artefacts at any particular place and time—whether adornment, or boasting of one's exploits, or marking a sacred site—they are bearers of meaning. Our ancestors long ago learnt to recognise and exploit the semiotic potential of the visual medium also.

the difference
between drawing
and writing

But this is not language; and the distinction is an important one. Painting a picture may be—perhaps always is—a form of communication, a symbolic act directed at other people. It may have a specific communicative purpose, such as recording past events or giving instructions on where and what to hunt. But this does not mean it is a form of language. If we use the word 'language' to refer to such activity, we are using it metaphorically, just as when we talk of music or mathematics as a kind of language. (There is no harm in this, obviously, provided we recognise the fact, and provided that we then have a clear way of indicating when we **are** talking about language in the primary sense of the term.)

12

Figure 2.1   Pictorial communication that is not writing

cathedrals

Governor Thomas Davey's proclamation to the Aborigines, Van Diemen's Land (Tasmania), 1816.

13

Let us use the term 'writing' in its exact sense, to mean a system of visual representation that is language. Such pictures, then, like those in Figure 2.1, may be a form of communication, but they are not a form of writing.

Children also learn to draw, usually some time after they have learnt to speak; and they then have to learn the distinction between drawing and writing. Here again there is a discontinuity: they have to 'leap' from one to the other, and the two are kept strictly apart. In the history of the human race, on the other hand, the line was not so clear. Drawing evolved gradually until it became writing.

From picture to character

Why do we say that a picture, even if it 'contains a message' or 'communicates something', is not writing?

First of all let us point out that the qualification 'even if it contains a message, or communicates something' really adds nothing at all, since any pictorial representation can be said to communicate something. Indeed, we are brought up to expect that it should do, as is shown by the common complaints of the picture-gazer: 'It doesn't mean anything to me'; compare also the language of art criticism, which makes frequent reference to what a picture 'conveys', its 'theme', 'symbolic significance', and so on.

Writing is a part of language: one form of expression.

But the question of whether something is writing or not can be answered in quite explicit terms. Writing is a part of language. More specifically, it is one kind of **expression** in language—an alternative to sound. We have said that a language consists of three strata: meaning, wording, and sound. We can now modify this, and say that a language consists of meaning, wording, and expression; and the expression may take the form **either** of sound **or** of writing.

One thing that follows from this is that writing can always be read aloud. If we look at a painting, or any other visual art form, we can describe it, make a commentary on it, 'say what it means'; but we cannot **read** it. We cannot decode it into wordings—because it is not an encoding of wordings in the first place. We could not list the elements of which it is made up, put them in a dictionary, and indicate how to pronounce them. They are not elements of a language.

The fact that we can make a clear distinction between what is writing and what is not does not mean there are no 'borderline cases'. There can always be instances that are mixed or indeterminate, however clearly defined the categories are in theory; and in the history of writing there must have been many, although none seems to have survived—which suggests that the transition from 'pre-writing' to writing may also have been fairly sudden.

how writing began: the coming together of two semiotic systems

But although we cannot document the process whereby writing first evolved, it is reasonably clear how it happened. Writing did not begin by somebody deciding to write language down instead of saying it aloud. It evolved from the coming together of two independent semiotic systems: language, on the one hand, and visual imagery on the other. Writing begins when pictures are **interpreted** as language.

14

Consider the shape shown in Figure 2.2. This is a picture incised on a bone, for purposes of divination, in China some time in the second millenium BC. It is a picture of a horse.

Figure 2.2   Earliest known form of Chinese character *horse*

No doubt the Chinese had been making pictorial representations of horses for a long time before that; none of them has survived. But at some time in this process, an important change took place in the way such a representation was interpreted. At first, it represented a 'horse': that is, the animal itself—or, more accurately, a member of that class of animals recognised as a distinct category in the culture.

By the time this bone was cut, however, it no longer represented a 'horse'; it represented *horse*, a word of the language. (That is to say, it represented the Chinese word pronounced [mɒ], which means 'horse' in English). It could now be read aloud.

Let us express this change of function in linguistic terms. **Functionally**, the shape (Figure 2.2) is no longer a picture; it has become a CHARACTER. Since that time, the shape of this particular character has varied considerably, as shown in Figure 2.3. But its function has remained the same. Figure 2.3(d) is the modern Chinese character for the word *ma* (now pronounced [mǎ]).

Figure 2.3   Evolution of the *horse* character

(a) 1000–800 BC   (b) c.500 BC   (c) 200 BC−1950 AD   (d) modern 'simplified'

The same process took place with hundreds of other pictorial representations. From being pictures, representing classes of objects, they became characters, representing words. The shapes themselves did not have to change; what changed was the way they were understood.

from pictures to characters

In time, of course, the visual shape does also tend to change. Once the visual symbol has become a character, and especially when this has happened in enough instances so that not just a few words here and there, but most of the words of the language, can be represented—in other words, once a writing **system** has evolved—then the shapes tend to become regularised and simplified, in ways that are strongly influenced by the materials that are used for writing on and with: incising on bone, casting in bronze, chiselling in clay, painting on silk, and so on. But the change of form is not a **necessary** consequence of the change of function. What creates writing is not the particular shapes that are

15

used; it is the way the shapes are interpreted.

This process, of reinterpreting representations of **things** as representations of **words**, took place—we presume independently—in three different parts of the world: (1) in south-west Asia and north-east Africa (Sumeria and Egypt), (2) in China, and (3) in central America (with the Mayans). We have no clear traces of the process itself; but then it would be difficult to recognise them if we had, since as already pointed out it does not necessarily involve changes in the forms themselves. All we can say for sure is that writing had effectively evolved by 4000 BC in Mesopotamia and the Nile delta, by 2000 BC in northern China, and by the turn of the era in what is now Mexico.

The Chinese system of writing

It is a little misleading to say, therefore, that writing evolved as 'language written down', since there were pictures long before there was writing, and one element in the origin of writing lies in the re-interpretation of pictures as characters. It is equally misleading, at the other extreme, to say that writing evolved 'independently of language', since it only becomes writing when the symbols are understood as linguistic symbols. A more accurate account would be to say that writing evolves when what are originally non-linguistic symbols get mapped on to the forms of the language.

However, not everything in language can be drawn a picture of. There are always forms ready at hand to serve as characters for *horse* and *mountain* and *tree*; but, if we were to start creating characters for English, we should find it difficult to produce a picture representing an *error*, or *to know*, or *dull*; to say nothing of words like *and*, *of*, *not*, and *the*. To be able to write some words but not others is already well worth doing; and it is likely that this was in fact the situation for quite some time, when writing was restricted to certain esoteric functions like divining. But as writing comes to be extended across a broader range of functions in the culture—recording achievements, marking property, keeping the calendar, making inventories, collecting taxes, conveying instructions, and so on—it inevitably evolves into a full WRITING SYSTEM: that is, a system in which all possible wordings in the language are able to be (more or less unambiguously) represented.

extending the functions of writing: towards a writing system

Let us see how this process took place in Chinese, as described with remarkable accuracy by a Chinese linguist of the first century AD named Xǔ Shèn. I have slightly modified his account, for clarity of exposition; but his theory was essentially correct. (See Figure 2.4 for the forms of the characters described.)

1. A picture is taken to serve as an indirect representation: for example, a picture of a tower for the word *high*; a man with arms and legs outstretched for the word *big*; a carpenter's square for the word *work*; a hand for the word *five*.
2. A new picture is created to give an iconic representation: for example, a dot above a line for the word *above*; one, two, three, and four parallel lines for (respectively) the words *one*, *two*, *three*, *four*; a cross (symbolising 'first unit' and 'first decade') for the word *ten*. There are not many of this type.

16

Figure 2.4 Development of Chinese characters

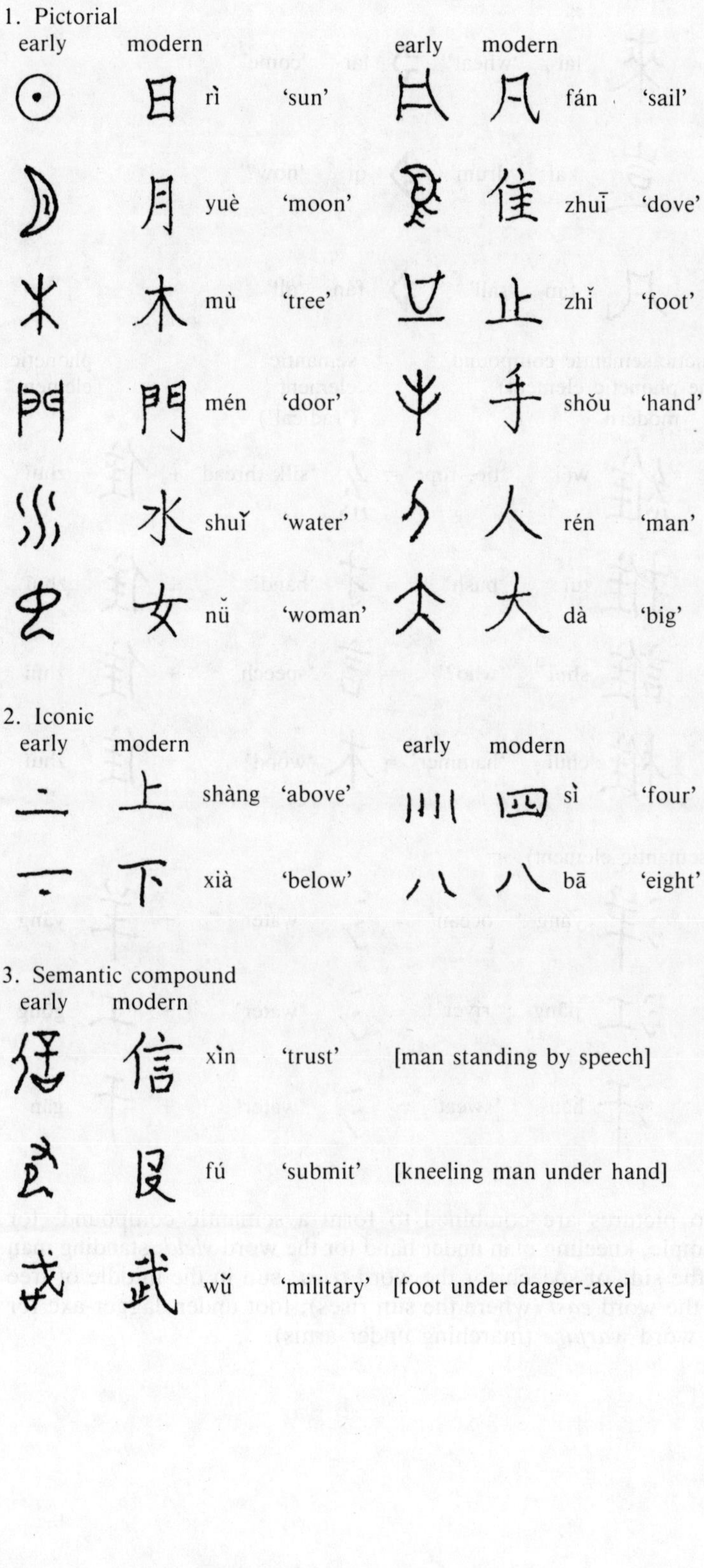

1. Pictorial

early	modern			early	modern		
⊙	日	rì	'sun'		凡	fán	'sail'
☽	月	yuè	'moon'		隹	zhuī	'dove'
木	木	mù	'tree'		止	zhǐ	'foot'
門	門	mén	'door'		手	shǒu	'hand'
水	水	shuǐ	'water'		人	rén	'man'
女	女	nǚ	'woman'		大	dà	'big'

2. Iconic

early	modern			early	modern		
二	上	shàng	'above'	川	四	sì	'four'
二	下	xià	'below'	八	八	bā	'eight'

3. Semantic compound

early	modern			
	信	xìn	'trust'	[man standing by speech]
	艮	fú	'submit'	[kneeling man under hand]
	武	wǔ	'military'	[foot under dagger-axe]

17

4. Phonetic transfer
early   modern

来 來 lái 'wheat' ⇒ lái 'come'

豈 豈 kǎi 'drum' ⇒ qǐ 'how?'

凡 凡 fán 'sail' ⇒ fán 'all'

5. Phonetic/semantic compound   semantic   phonetic
   (same phonetic element)   element   element
   early   modern   ('radical')

維 維 wéi 'tie, rope' = 幺 'silk thread' + 隹 zhuī

推 推 tuī 'push' = 扌 'hand' + 隹 zhuī

誰 誰 shuí 'who?' = 言 'speech' + 隹 zhuī

椎 椎 chuí 'hammer' = 木 'wood' + 隹 zhuī

(same semantic element)

洋 洋 yáng 'ocean' = 氵 'water' + 羊 yáng

江 江 jiāng 'river' = 氵 'water' + 工 gōng

汗 汗 hàn 'sweat' = 氵 'water' + 干 gān

3. Two pictures are combined to form a semantic compound: for example, kneeling man under hand for the word *yield*; standing man by the side of speech for the word *trust*; sun in the middle of tree for the word *east* (where the sun rises); foot under dagger-axe for the word *warfare* (marching under arms).

In those listed up to this point there has been no connection made with the **sound** of the word. Two further strategies were adopted that involved taking account of sound, either (4) instead of or (5) as well as meaning.

what happened when Chinese writing evolved

4. A picture is 'borrowed' for a word of similar sound, by a process of phonetic transfer: for example, the character for wheat, Old Chinese [ləg], for the word *come* (same pronunciation); the character for *war drum*, Old Chinese [kʹər] for the word *how?* [kʹiər]; the character for *sail*, Old Chinese [biwăm], for the word *all* (same pronunciation); the character for *flute*, Old Chinese [ŋiăn], for the word *speech* (same pronunciation).
5. Two pictures are combined, one indicating the sound, the other indicating the meaning, to give a semantic-phonetic compound (a combination of the principles of 1 and 4 above): for example, the character for *dove*, Old Chinese [ţiwər], used as phonetic element and combined with (a) the character for *silk thread* to represent the word *tie, rope* [diwər], (b) with the character for *hand* to represent the word *push* [tʹwər], (c) with the character for *speech* to represent the word *who?* [d̥iwər], (d) with the character for *tree, wood*, to represent the word *hammer* [dʹiwər]. More than three quarters of all the characters used in the modern language are of this type.

The Chinese writing system, therefore, is a CHARACTERY; its symbols are characters. This means that they represent the wording of the language: the entities they stand for are words (or, more accurately, MORPHEMES, the smallest units of wording—to give an analogy from English, if the word *kindness* was written with a charactery there would be one character for the morpheme *kind* and another for the morpheme *ness*).

The technical term for a character, indicating its function in the language, is LOGOGRAM. Despite popular belief, characters are **not** ideograms, and Chinese writing is **not** ideographic. Characters stand for words, not for meanings. They are unambiguous when read aloud, and synonyms are not written alike; whereas if they were ideographic, synonyms would have to be written alike and there would be no unambiguous readings.

Chinese writing not 'ideographic' but 'logographic'

This kind of writing system is appropriate for the Chinese language. It is neither more nor less advanced than other writing systems, such as that of English; but the English writing system is different in a fundamental respect. In English, the written symbols represent the language not at the level of wording but at the level of sound. The next section describes how this system came about.

From ancient Egyptian to English

The first writing system developed in ancient Egypt was a charactery. Its characters are known as 'hieroglyphs', meaning 'sacred carving'.

Starting many centuries earlier, hieroglyphic writing had developed along the path that we have described above for Chinese (see Figure 2.5(a)). The principle of phonetic transfer was established by the third

19

millennium BC, and semantic indicators were added to form phonetic-semantic compounds (see Figure 2.5(b)).

Figure 2.5(a)   Egyptian hieroglyphics, showing also development as syllabic symbols

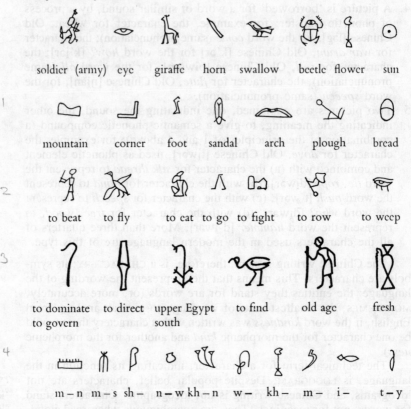

2.5a. Hieroglyphic word signs. 1, symbols representing things shown 2, ideographs representing actions associated with things shown; 3, symbols representing abstract ideas; 4, hieroglyphic bi-consonantal signs.

At this point, however, the route taken was different from that in Chinese. In Old Chinese, all words were monosyllables; so there was never a case where one word was made up of the sounds of two or more others. In Old Egyptian, however, words could vary in the number of their syllables; so it frequently happened that one long word could be broken down into a number of syllables each of which was also a word, although quite unrelated to it; for example, the word *khesteb* 'turquoise' sounded like *khes* 'to stop' plus *teb* 'a pig'. This is the principle on which the game of charades is based, where we act out, for example, *can*, *knee*, *ball*, and then *cannibal*.

To write a polysyllabic word of this kind, it would be a natural step to break it down into its component parts. But notice that these 'parts' are not morphemes; they are syllables. The word *snowball* consists of the **morphemes** *snow* + *ball*; if we write it with the character

Figure 2.5(b) Determinatives in hieroglyphic writing

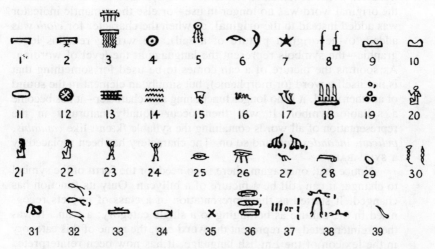

1. Heaven, Sky, Ceiling, what is above. 2. Night sky with a star hanging like a lamp from it, darkness, night. 3. (above) Sky slipping down over its four supports, storm, hurricane; (below) rain or dew falling from the sky. 4. Sun, the sun-god Ra, day period, time in general. 5. Shine, rise (of a luminary), being of light. 6. Moon, month. 7. Star, morning star, hour, time for prayer, pray. 8. Flourish, blooming, year, time in general, last year of a King's reign. 9. Foreign country, desert. 10. Mountain. 11. Island. 12. City, town. 13. Nome, District. 14. Water, watery mass of the sky. 15. Skin, hide. 16. Worm. 17. Plant, vegetable, herb, dried up. 18. Field, garden. 19. Grain, corn. 20. Man, first person sing. 21. Woman, first and second person sing. 22. God or divine person. 23. Pray, worship, adore, entreat, praise. 24. High, lofty, exalt, make merry. 25. To see. 26. To weep, tear, grief. 27. Hair (of men and animals), bald, lack, want, lacuna (in manuscripts), colour, complexion. 28. Phallus, front, male, masculine, procreate. 29. Women, godessess, cities. 30. Sweet, pleasant. 31. Incense. 32. Roll of papyrus, tie up, bind together, come to an end. 33. Roll of papyrus (tied round the middle), book, deed, document, register, group together, abstract ideas. 34. Oval round a royal name, known as *cartouche*. 35. Pair of tallies, count, tally, reckon, pass by, depart. 36. Bread, cake. 37. Sign of the plural 38. Negation, no, not, nothing, lack, want, need. 39. Horn.

for *snow* plus the character for *ball*, we have not changed the **function** of the symbols. But *cannibal* does not consist of the **morphemes** *can* + *knee* + *ball*; these are quite different morphemes, which happen to be represented by its component syllables.

If we choose to write *cannibal* with the symbols for *can*, *knee*, and *ball*, we hardly need the semantic indicators. Taken by itself, the character for the word *can* 'container', if transferred to stand for the word *can* 'am able', might conceivably cause problems of understanding. But a string of characters for the words *can* 'container', *knee*, and *ball* would make no sense at all, unless each was reinterpreted as standing for the **syllables** /kæn/, /ni/, /bɔl/ which taken together would make up the word *cannibal*.

But once this step has been taken, the whole nature of the writing system becomes transformed. As long as there is, in principle, a separate

the direction taken in ancient Egypt: towards the representation of the sounds of language

21

character for each **word**, as was the case in Chinese (where phonetic transfers **without** semantic elements were confined to instances where the original word was no longer in use—or else the semantic indicator was added instead to the **original**, as when the character for *cloth* was added to the original picture of a sail), the writing remains logographic—the symbols represent the language at the level of wording. As soon as the picture of a can comes to be used for something that is **not** itself a word (or morpheme), but simply an element in the **sound** of another word, it is no longer functioning as a character—it has become a syllabic symbol. It will then occur equally naturally in the representation of all words containing the syllable /kæn/, like *cannabis*, *pelican*, *incandescent*, and so on. The charactery has been replaced by a SYLLABARY.

Notice that, once again, there is no need for the **form** of the symbol to change; it can still be a picture of a billycan. Only its function has changed. It started as the representation of a **class of objects** recognised in the culture as belonging to a single category: a 'can'. It was then reinterpreted, to represent the **word** *can*, the name of this category in the lexicon of the English language. It has now been reinterpreted over again, so that it represents the **syllable** /kæn/, which is an element of English phonology. When this change has flowed through the whole writing system, the symbols no longer stand for words but for sounds. The script has become a phonological one.

Charactery, syllabary, alphabet

As a matter of fact, this change never did take place fully in the Egyptian writing system, which always retained some of the features of a charactery. But it did take place in languages whose speakers borrowed their writing system from the Egyptian, of which the one that is significant for our purposes is Phoenician.

Phoenician: the development of a syllabary

Phoenician was a Semitic language, like modern Arabic and Hebrew. The Phoenicians took over a small number of Egyptian symbols and used them as syllabic signs. Thus the Phoenician word for 'water' was *mem* (cf. Hebrew *mayim*); the Phoenicians took the Egyptian character for *water* and used it to represent the syllable /ma/—keeping the word *mem* as the **name** of the symbol (as we have **names** for the letters of our alphabet: /ei/, /bi/, /si/, /di/, etc).

Similarly, the Phoenician word for 'snake' -was *nun*; so they borrowed the Egyptian *snake* character and used it to represent the syllable /na/—calling the symbol itself *nun*. They borrowed about thirty symbols in all, and listed them a fixed order: first came the Egyptian 'ox' character, Phoenician word ʔ*aleph* (from which we get our word *elephant*), beginning with a glottal stop, and hence used for the syllable /ʔa/; and second the Egyptian character for 'house', Phoenician *beth* (cf. Hebrew *beyth*), used for the syllable /ba/.

This kind of script was well suited to the Phoenician language, in which, as in modern Arabic, the root of a word is a sequence of (usually three) consonants; the vowels in between will vary (along with affixes before and after) to signal grammatical categories of person, tense, number, and so on. So, for example, the consonant sequence /k-t-b/ means 'write, book', and yields a large number of words such as *katab* 'he wrote', *niktib* 'we write', *kitab* 'book', *kateb* 'clerk', *maktub* 'written', and so on. In a similar way the words *Islam*, *Muslim*, and *salaam* all come from the same root /s-l-m/ meaning 'peace'. In a language of this type, it is natural to have a writing system in which the symbol stands for a consonant plus **any** following vowel. The reader can be left to supply the appropriate vowel from the context; or alternatively, the vowel can be indicated by some additional diacritic, with perhaps the convention that if it is not marked then it is to be read as /-a/. There have been various forms of Semitic script, but all have been based on this kind of syllabic principle.

Next in line were the Greeks, who took over the Phoenician symbols and used them to write Greek. Greek, however, is a very different kind of language, in which vowels are just as much a fixed part of the word root as consonants are; moreover, there can be whole clusters of consonants in a single syllable, as in the word /straŋks/ meaning 'throat'. A syllabary, therefore, would be quite inappropriate. So the Greeks used each symbol to stand just for the consonant, without any following vowels; and they then added separate symbols for the vowels, either using Phoenician symbols for which they had no other use (like aleph— there was no glottal stop in Greek, so they adopted this symbol for the vowel /a/) or making up new ones for themselves. The result was an ALPHABET (so called because the Greeks also borrowed the Phoenician names for the symbols they took over, and these were the first two in order).

Greek: the development of an alphabet

An alphabet resembles a syllabary in that its symbols stand for sounds, not words; but they stand for smaller units of sound—not syllables, but PHONEMES. In principle, one letter represents one phoneme; and that was more or less the case with the ancient Greek alphabet. This was then adapted to various dialects of Greek; and one of the dialect scripts was in turn borrowed by the Romans, who again adapted it slightly, left out some letters they did not need, and used it to write Latin. This Latin alphabet is essentially what we use for English today.

Table 2.1 summarises the various kinds of writing system.

Table 2.1 Kinds of writing system

Level of language represented:	lexico-grammatical (wording)	phonological (sound)	
Linguistic unit represented:	word/morpheme	syllable	phoneme
Type of symbol:	character ('logogram')	syllabic sign	letter
Type of script:	charactery	syllabary	alphabet

As usual, the categories themselves are clearly defined; but any given instance may be mixed or intermediate. Thus the Semitic scripts are not, in fact, pure syllabaries; they are in a sense intermediate between a syllabary and an alphabet. A stricter case of a syllabary would be the Japanese *kana* script, adapted from Chinese characters. And our

summary of the different kinds of writing system

English writing system is certainly not purely phonemic.

There is a great deal of variation among different languages; but one thing is common to all: all languages are highly complex. When they are written down, the writing system has to be open-ended and flexible to accommodate the richness and complexity. When people try to design scripts, they usually make the mistake of making them too pure, and hence too rigid. When scripts evolve (which nearly always starts with borrowing—as we have seen, writing was developed independently in, at most, four contexts in human history, and even among these there may have been some transmission), they gradually adapt themselves to the needs of the particular language—which means they become somewhat messy and indeterminate. A writing system needs to be reformed now and again, because languages are always changing, whereas scripts, once codified, tend to stay as they are until someone takes positive action. But attempts to create ideal writing systems are bound to fail, because it is impossible to define what an ideal script should achieve—and if one could define such an ideal, it would certainly be impossible to attain.

A note on 'ideograms'

The symbols of all natural writing systems began as pictures. This is as true of the letters of our alphabet as it is of the characters of Chinese. Every time you write the word *man*, you are drawing three pictures—water, an ox head, and a snake (see Figure 2.6).

Figure 2.6 Evolution of letters m, a, n

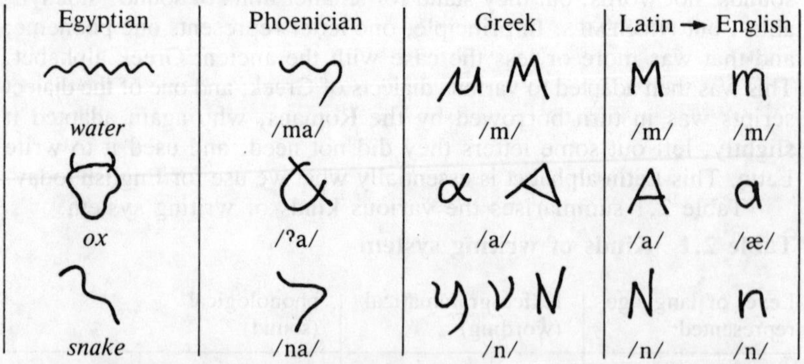

Egyptian	Phoenician	Greek	Latin → English
~~ *water*	ﾁ /ma/	μ M /m/	M m /m/ /m/
𓄿 *ox*	& /ʔa/	α ◁ /a/	A a /a/ /æ/
ʓ *snake*	ϟ /na/	ꭹ ν N /n/	N n /n/ /n/

Functionally, on the other hand, no written symbol is ever a pictogram; in that sense, a 'pictographic script' is a contradiction in terms. If a symbol is part of a writing system, it must represent some element of a language; in that case it is not **functioning** as a picture.

What about the term 'ideogram'? I have avoided using that term because it is not at all clear what it means; it is used rather inconsistently in most discussions of language. But it is possible to make sense of it. If we refer back to the diagram in Figure 1.1, we can see that the level of representation of the writing systems so far described has been either lexico-grammatical or phonological. Nothing has been said of writing representing the semantic elements of a language.

As a general phenomenon, a semantic writing system would be an impossibility. The semantic systems of natural languages are so complex, with so many intersecting dimensions of meaning involved, that they could not be reduced to writing—for exactly the same reason, in fact, that they cannot be expressed in a protolanguage. The only possible writing systems are those whose symbols represent, as a general principle, either wording or sound.

Can a writing system have symbols standing for meanings?

In the seventeenth century there were various attempts, in England, Holland, and France, to create semantically based writing systems, attempts that were encouraged by a misunderstanding of the nature of Chinese characters. Scholars hoped in this way to produce a writing system that would be the same for all languages, and would serve to express the new scientific knowledge and new ways of reasoning. These schemes did not work; but a great deal was learnt about language in the process. One of the by-products, 150 years later, was *Roget's Thesaurus*.

But it is possible for a script to embody some use of semantic representations, as a minor theme; and perhaps the clearest example of this is Japanese. Until the fifth century AD, Japanese was not written down; then there were two large-scale invasions from China, as a result of which Japanese borrowed from Chinese both the writing system and a large amount of vocabulary. Japanese, however, is a very different kind of language from Chinese (to which it is also quite unrelated— Japanese is recognised to be an Altaic language, probably with an earlier substratum of Austronesian), and a charactery is entirely unsuited to it. What does suit it is a syllabary, and after a century or two the Japanese modified and simplified two sets of Chinese characters to create a syllabic writing system of their own.

By this time, however, there were many Chinese words in the language, which although they **could** be written in the syllabary (their phonology having become adapted to Japanese) were also entirely at home in charactery; so the Japanese retained the characters and used them side by side with their own syllabic signs. Various patterns grew up, the predominant one being Chinese characters ('kanji') for the lexical roots and Japanese syllabic signs ('kana') for the affixes and for grammatical words.

In this process, however, the characters were not confined to words borrowed from Chinese; they were also used to represent the roots of native Japanese words that were similar in meaning—the same character often being used for more than one Japanese word. Thus, for example, the character for the Chinese word *měi* 'beautiful' (Middle Chinese pronunciation [mjwi]) stands in Japanese for the following: (1) the word *mjwi* borrowed—twice, from different dialects—into Japanese, now pronounced either [bi] or [mi]; (2) the native Japanese word *utsukushii*, meaning 'beautiful'; and (3) the native Japanese word *yoi* meaning 'good'.

some features of Japanese writing

From the Chinese point of view, a character is tied absolutely to a particular word. From the Japanese point of view, however, that same character may stand for three or four different words, unrelated to each other in sound or form but related to each other in meaning. In other words, it tends to have for them a semantic as well as a lexico-grammatical significance: part logogram, part what we might call 'semogram'. It is in this sense that the Japanese themselves often refer to their writing as 'ideographic'. The term is inaccurate, since it is not 'ideas' but meanings that are being represented; but at least it makes an intelligible use of the term, so there is no reason why we should particularly reject it.

Some Japanese claim that it is because of their mixed script, partly phonological (the syllabary) and partly lexico-grammatical with a dash of semantic (the charactery), that they have little or no dyslexia in the population. It is impossible to prove this one way or the other; but it is an interesting idea—the virtues of a script that has something in it for everyone.

The English writing system

There is a tendency for mixed languages to get mixed scripts. Japanese is one example; English is another.

Like Japanese, English has been through a great deal of outside influence. After the English overran Britain, their language was strongly influenced by the native Celtic languages—hardly at all in vocabulary, but quite considerably in some aspects of its grammar. Next it was successively invaded by Norwegian, Danish, and Norman French; then in the Renaissance, it took over massive doses of Latin and Greek, not only lexical roots but also large numbers of affixes and the morphological processes that went with them.

Like every other European language, English inherited an alphabetic writing system; and after a few letters had been added (Latin had a very simple phonological system, so its alphabet is rather impoverished from the point of view of most other languages), it was excellently suited to the writing of Old English (Anglo-Saxon). The Norman French scribes destroyed some of its good qualities, by refusing to write the symbols they did not recognise; but what really perturbed it were two phenomena that took place in the language itself. One was the great internal upheaval that took place in Middle English (1100–1500), when the language changed extremely quickly and a dialectally mixed standard variety evolved; the other was the inflow of Graeco-Romance elements from 1450 onwards, already referred to above.

The effect on the writing system was likewise twofold. Just when the spelling was becoming standardised, it had suddenly grown rather archaic; the language had changed, and the spelling continued to reflect its earlier phonological patterns. Secondly, the Latin and Greek borrowings brought with them new phonological patterns from outside that had somehow to be reconciled with the native ones—while at the same time the Latin (and Latinised Greek) spelling was retained largely unaltered. There were thus two partially distinct phonological systems, compatible but not homogenised, each represented by different spelling conventions neither of which was particularly appropriate.

The French, who had similar problems, tackled them by setting up an Academy, which would legislate about the language and its orthography; the result was a writing system that is consistent but massively archaic. The English, equally characteristically, let things take their course, and ended up with a writing system that looks incredibly muddled, but in which the superficial messiness hides a rather effective compromise between the old and the new, the native and the foreign. It is far from perfect; but it has many virtues—not the least of which is that it is quietly neutral among all the various native and non-native forms of English that are now spoken around the world. When it was confined to England, and other English-speaking areas of the British Isles, it had already proved its ability to represent the various local accents of standard English. (These are not the original dialects, which have now largely disappeared except in some rural areas; they are vastly different and have their own orthographies.) Now, it serves not only the 'first language' English of Australia, New Zealand, South Africa, the Caribbean, Canada, and the United States but also the 'second language' English of many other parts of the world—South Asia, many countries of Africa, Singapore, and the South Pacific.

the evolution of the English writing system

Like the Japanese script, English writing ought to be impossible to learn; but—again like Japanese—it is not. Its mixed character is also what makes it accessible. In the first place, to the extent that it is a phonological script, it is not phonemic. It allows various other principles to override the phonemic one. For example, it writes *photograph* in *photograph*, *photography*, and *photographic* all alike, even though their phonemic structure is very different; and similarly with many hundreds of other related sets. It allows Anglo-Saxon and Graeco-Romance words to have different spelling conventions rather than forcing one to adapt—incongruously, as it would be—to the other. It embodies strange, minor, but very useful conventions of its own, like the two-, three-, and four-letter rule (grammatical words can have two letters, lexical words must have at least three, and proper names, at least four; cf. the well-known example *Mr Inne is in the inn*). But at the same time, it works by tendencies and not by rules—which is exactly how language works as well.

In the second place, it is not entirely phonological, but also partly logographic. There are many sets of words in English that are pronounced in an identical fashion, but are kept apart in the spelling. There is no necessity for this, of course; but it is useful for two reasons. One is the dialectal neutrality referred to above. For example, in my own dialect *paw*, *poor*, *pour*, and *pore* are all identical, whereas for many speakers of English there are two or even three different syllables among them; on the other hand, we distinguish *higher* and *hire*, which many English speakers pronounce alike. The spelling allows for all sorts of different groupings.

Some features of English writing: not limited to any one kind of English; not purely based on sound; operates with tendencies not rules.

The other reason is that, although such homonymy causes no trouble in speech, written language is not spoken language written down. It has a life of its own, in which it is useful to be able to use words without the same environmental cushioning that is characteristic of speech. When we talk, there is always a context; it poses no great problem that many words are pronounced alike. In writing, however, where the whole object is to get away from dependence on the immediate environment while still remaining unambiguous, it is useful to be able to put up a notice saying *wait for pause after whole lessons* without at the same time saying *weight four paws after hole lessens*. With a purely phonological script, the written text makes the same demand on the context as the spoken one.

Up to this point, we have been exploring the origin of speech and the development and nature of writing. It is now time to turn to the exploration of written language.

Chapter 3
Written language

Codified and codable expressions

Up to this point we have been assuming that whatever is spoken can also be written—that writing is simply an alternative form of expression to speech. We now need to examine this assumption a little more closely.

In the broadest sense, the assumption can be allowed to stand. That is to say, a writing system is capable of **representing** all possible wordings in the language: (1) by providing ready-made ('codified') expressions, for the majority of elements, and (2) by providing the means of creating ('coding') expressions for elements that are not already codified—new borrowings and coinings, an individual writer's neologisms, mistakes (for example, children and foreigners), and the like. So English, for example, contains (1) recognised **spellings** for the great majority of its words, and (2) recognised **principles** of spelling that can be applied where the spellings do not yet exist.

At an earlier stage in the language, the early Modern English period when standard English was emerging and printing had just begun, there was much less codification; writers used a variety of different spellings. But if principle (1) had not yet been generally applied, principle (2) held good: the variation was within the limits of tacitly agreed practice, and there was no problem of intelligibility—texts could be read without difficulty (and the literacy rate among adults was for that time extremely high; it has been estimated that in the fifteenth century over half the population could read). We tend to take it for granted that spelling should be totally uniform; but there is no compelling reason why it should be, provided the principles are clear. We understand each other's spoken language throughout the English-speaking world, unhampered by the wide variation in dialect—because all dialects are underlain by what is, by and large, a single phonological system. The same principle will work for writing.

As a rule, however, writing systems tend to engender conformity once they come into general use; partly for convenience, and partly because the development of writing tends to be associated with norma-

English writing provides (1) standardised spellings for old words and (2) principles for spelling new ones.

tive processes anyway—the emergence of a literary, religious, learned or general 'standard' language that is highly valued (and therefore to be kept 'pure') and that may be deliberately planned and even legislated for. The conformity that is expected of the language is expected also of the way it is written; indeed it may exist primarily as a written language, not used in speech except when read aloud, so that uniform writing becomes the main symbol of its identity. And when learning to write becomes institutionalised in education, this further strengthens the pressure to conform.

Writing systems tend towards uniformity.

So writing systems tend towards uniformity, towards providing codified expressions for all the established wordings of the language whether in characters, in syllabic or alphabetic spellings, or in some intermediate or composite forms. And for anything that is not codified, they provide general principles whereby expressions can be created. Does that mean, however, that writing incorporates all the features of speech?

Clearly it does not. There are various aspects of spoken language that have no counterpart in writing: rhythm, intonation, degrees of loudness, variation in voice quality ('tamber'), pausing, and phrasing—as well as indexical features by which we recognise that it is Mary talking and not Jane, the individual characteristics of a particular person's speech.

The question that naturally arises is whether these omissions are accidental—whether these are features that it is simply difficult to write down, or difficult to write in one particular kind of script; or whether they are in some sense motivated—there is some good reason why writing systems should not incorporate features of this kind. The answer—as usual in linguistics—is that it is a bit of both.

What writing leaves out

It is true that it is difficult to write down features of this kind. Or rather, it is not intrinsically difficult; but it is difficult to do in such a way that they can be combined with the representation of words.

what writing leaves out: prosodic and paralinguistic features

These features of spoken language are known as PROSODIC and PARALINGUISTIC features. The difference between these two categories is as follows. Prosodic features are part of the linguistic system; they carry systematic contrasts in meaning, just like other resources in the grammar, and what distinguishes them from these other resources (such as word endings) is that they spread across extended portions of speech, like an intonation contour, for example. Paralinguistic features also extend over stretches of varying length; but they are not systematic— they are not part of the grammar, but rather additional variations by which the speaker signals the import of what he is saying. INDEXICAL features, by contrast, are not part of the language at all, but simple properties of the individual speaker. It may be helpful to tabulate these (see Table 3.1).

They are difficult to represent in writing precisely because they do not belong at any particular point. Writing is inherently linear and segmental: it takes the form of a sequence of discrete elements, and

Table 3.1 Features not embodied in wording

Status	linguistic		non-linguistic
Description	systematic (grammatical/ phonological features of the [English] language)	non-systematic (vocal and gestural variations that carry meaning in [English] speech)	individual (patterns outside the individual's control that display his/her identity)
Technical name	prosodies	paralanguage	indexical features
Principal types	intonation (tonicity and tone) rhythm 'phrasing' and pausing	tamber (breathy, creaky etc. voice qualities) tempo loudness facial and bodily gestures	pitch range (soprano—bass) resonance tension [+individual preferences for certain prosodic and paralinguistic patterns]

although these elements may be grouped in various ways (see below on spacing and punctuation), they are still essentially linear configurations, like a line of dominoes forming a streak. It is difficult to superimpose on a structure of this kind a representation of other patterns that are of greater and highly variable extent. It could be done, of course; an analogy is found in musical notation, where words denoting features of this kind are written above the staff, words such as *andante*, *crescendo*, *con moto*—sometimes accompanied, or substituted, by other symbols such as <. It would be possible to add signals of this kind above or below the line of type, or to incorporate them in a special box at the beginning; and there is one kind of written language where something of the sort is done, namely dramatic dialogue with its 'stage directions' such as [*angrily*] or [*with great condescension*]. But this has never become a feature of written language in general.

This suggests that there is some reason why not. The reason can be found in the different functions of speech and writing. David Abercrombie, in his discussion of the work of the great eighteenth-century phonetician Joshua Steele, put it like this:

> The letters in which language is normally written do not represent more than a part of spoken language. Writing, of course, is perfectly intelligible without these missing ingredients. But then writing is a medium for language in its own right, and though it is, in the last analysis, constructed on the basis of spoken language, the aim of writing is not, usually, to represent actual spoken utterances which have occurred.
>
> (Abercrombie 1965, p.36)

31

why these features
are not found in
writing

What then is the nature of these 'missing ingredients' that writing can do without? Essentially they are the on-the-spot features of language, the things that tie it to the particular moment and context of speaking. The speaker's state of mind, the reservations and doubts he or she may be feeling, the hesitations, the weight given to different parts of an argument—these will have no place in most uses of written language. Why?—because in its core functions, writing is not anchored in the here-and-now. The particular conditions that obtain at the time of writing are not going to be present to the reader anyway, who is usually at some distance from the writer both in time and place; so much of the message that is contained in the rhythm and tamber of speech would simply be irrelevant. It might even be claimed that they are not there: that in the composing of a written text, the writer just does not make the choices in meaning that are expressed by these devices. If this is so, then it is not merely that writing 'leaves out' these features of discourse, but that, if it is written discourse, they are never there to be put in. They are inherently features that are present only in spoken language.

Having made this case, we must now proceed to challenge and, in part, destroy it. It is true that written language is very different from spoken language. It has different functions, different contexts, and consequently it 'means' in very different ways. At the same time, it is **not** true that all the features listed above (as 'prosodic and paralinguistic') have no place or significance in the written mode. For one thing, 'written' and 'spoken' do not form a simple dichotomy; there are all sorts of writing and all sorts of speech, many of which display features characteristic of the other medium. For another thing, different people vary, and the same person varies on different occasions, in the 'implication of utterance' that is given to writing—at one moment you may be talking to yourself as you write, while at another your writing may be as deadpan as if you were doing a crossword puzzle. And finally, certain prosodic features are accidental properties of the particular language: for example, some of the meanings that are expressed by intonation in English are expressed by particles in Vietnamese or in German; so in those languages these meanings get written down, whereas in English they do not.

So the omission of prosodic features from written language is, in some respects and under certain circumstances, a genuine deficiency. There is, on the other hand, a device that is used in order partially to overcome this deficiency; this is the device of punctuation.

Punctuation

Greek alphabetic writing began as a string of letters, without spaces and without punctuation. The first line usually went from left to right; when the writer reached the end of the line, he went down about the height of one letter and went back along the line from right to left; then left to right again, and so on with alternate lines. A passage of English written in this continuous zigzag fashion would look like this:

onethingwascertainthatthewhitekittenhadhadnothingtodowithititwa
cafstignivahneebdahnettiketihwehtrofyleritnetluafsnettikkcalbehts
ewashedbytheoldcatforthelastquarterofanhourandbearingitprettyw
feihcsimehtnidnahynadahevahtndluoctitahteesuoyosgniredisnoclle

Step by step, over the centuries, innovations were introduced that eventually led to writing in our modern form:

1. The line direction was standardised, the Greeks settling on a left-to-right succession (while the Phoenicians opted to go the other way).
2. Spaces were introduced between words.
3. A punctuation mark, the stop, was introduced to mark off sentences.
4. Capital (upper case) and small (lower case) letters were systematically distinguished, with capitals having various special functions.
5. Special symbols were brought in to indicate linkages, interpolations, and omissions (hyphen, parenthesis, apostrophe).
6. Other, more detailed punctuation marks were added: comma, colon, semicolon, dash.
7. Further special purpose symbols came into the system: quotation marks (single and double 'inverted commas'), question mark, exclamation mark.

Collectively, these symbols have three kinds of function. One is boundary marking. The grammar of every language is organised through a small hierarchy of units of different size: in English, sentences, clauses, phrases, words, and morphemes. Gradually the writing system has come to take account of these.

functions of punctuation (1): boundary marking

The most distinctive, words and sentences, were the first to be recognised: words marked off by spaces, sentences by full stops. Subsequently, the writing system provided for intermediate units by means of colon and comma: comma for weaker boundaries, colon for stronger ones. Both can be used to separate clauses, the difference serving to indicate internal bracketing, as in Figure 3.1. The comma is also used to mark off phrases, and even words, if the occasion demands: for example, for an afterthought, or in a list. A very late distinction was made between a colon and a semicolon, the colon having a special CATAPHORIC (forward-referring) implication.

Figure 3.1 Bracketing effect of punctuation

$$[\{(\ \ ),\ (\ \ )\};\ \{(\ \ ),\ (\ \ ),\ (\ \ )\}].$$

The second function of the symbols is status marking. It is not enough to show that a sentence has finished; it is also important to indicate its speech function—is it a statement, question, or neither? So there is a contrast between full stop, for statements; question mark, for questions; and exclamation mark, used for a mixed bag of speech functions including commands, suggestions, offers, exclamations, calls, and greetings. The last six all share the negative property that they are **not** exchanges of information; the speaker is either exchanging goods-and-services (offers, suggestions, and commands; for example, *I'll help you! Let's be friends! Go home!*), expressing his or her own attitude (exclamations, for example, *What a mess!*), or establishing social contact (calls and greetings, for example, *Bob! Hullo there!*)

functions of punctuation (2): status marking

The signs *?* and *!* were introduced in medieval times. The question mark was the letter *q*, the initial letter of Latin *quaestio* 'question',

33

reversed and placed above the stop; the exclamation mark was an *i* above an *o*, representing the Latin exclamation *io* in the form of a single symbol.

The other symbol of status is the quotation mark. This is used to ascribe some part of the text to someone other than the writer: either a quotation (for example, something said by a character in a narrative) or a citation (for example, a word or phrase cited as an example, or a highlighted word such as a technical term). It comes in two forms, single and double, and is one of the most inconsistently used of all the punctuation marks. Modern editors typically use the doubled version for a quote inside a quote, for example:

'It says ''Bough-wough!'' ' cried Daisy.

Another tradition has double quotation marks for sayings and single ones for thoughts. But the two have often been used more or less interchangeably.

We can then recognise a third, rather minor function, about which it is difficult to generalise, but which we could perhaps label vaguely as 'relation markers'. This includes (1) the hyphen, which signals a link across a space (either a word space or line end), showing either that two words are to be taken as forming a compound, or that two letter sequences separated by a line break (typically, two morphemes) are to be taken as forming a word; (2) the dash, which signals that the following element is to be taken in apposition with the preceding one; (3) parentheses, which indicate that the enclosed element is a kind of sub-routine, a loop off the main track of the sentence; (4) the apostrophe, which is a kind of place holder signifying either that a letter has been omitted (to recognise an informal variant, as in the negative finites *didn't*, *won't*, etc.) or, by convention, that a noun is possessive (*Fred's*, *Hans'*, *the girls'*).

The actual printed version of the sentence written above in boustrophedon fashion (continuous zigzag) is as follows:

> One thing was certain, that the white kitten had had nothing to do with it:—it was the black kitten's fault entirely. For the *white* kitten had been having its face washed by the old cat for the last quarter of an hour (and bearing it pretty well, considering); so you see that it *couldn't* have had any hand in the mischief.
> (L. Carroll, *Through the Looking Glass*, Bodley Head, London, 1974, ch.1)

Table 3.2 summarises the categories of punctuation in English.

How punctuation relates to grammar and phonology

As far as the use of the status markers is concerned, practice is fairly consistent. In the first place, there are many registers (functional varieties) of written English that consist simply of successions of statements, without other speech functions and without PROJECTIONS ('direct' quoting, or citation); in these registers there is no call for status symbols other than the full stop.

functions of punctuation (3): relation marking

Table 3.2 Categories of English punctuation

Type	Feature represented			Symbol	
	general	specific		name	form
Boundary markers	grammatical units	word		space	(#)
		phrase; weaker clause		comma	,
		clause	closing	semicolon	;
			opening	colon	:
		sentence		full stop	.
Status markers	speech function	information exchange	statement		
			question	question mark	?
		other functions	command, offer, suggestion, exclamation, call, greeting	exclamation mark	!
	projection	quotation, citation	first order; or meaning	single quote	' '
			second order; or wording	double quote	" "
Relation markers	any unit	apposition		dash	—
		digression		parenthesis	( )
	(compound) word	linkage		hyphen	-
	possessive, negative	omission		apostrophe	'

In the second place, in those registers that are not confined to unprojected statements, such as dramatic dialogue and narrative fiction, there is little uncertainty about where these other categories occur. People tend to agree on what a question is.

The principal variation is in the use of the exclamation mark, which some writers are much freer with than others; and in the distinction between single and double inverted commas, which tends to be purely arbitrary.

There is some uncertainty about the punctuation of 'free indirect speech'; but the preference seems to be for punctuating it as if it was the writer who was speaking:

> Alice rubbed her eyes, and looked again. She couldn't make out what had happened at all. Was she in a shop? And was that really—was it really a sheep that was sitting on the other side of the counter?
>
> (L. Carroll, *Through the Looking Glass*, ch.5)

But the boundary markers allow for systematic variation; and in order to understand this we need to ask how they had come into the writing system in the first place.

Language remains unconscious until it is written down.

As long as language is not written down, people remain largely unconscious of it. As Franz Boas observed many years ago:

> It would seem that the essential difference between linguistic phenomena and other ethnological phenomena is, that the linguistic classifications never rise into consciousness . . . the categories which are formed always remain unconscious . . . Cases are rare in which a people have begun to speculate about linguistic categories.
>
> (Boas (n.d.), pp.56, 59)

When language comes to be written down, people become aware of it; they start to speculate about it, and this is the origin of linguistics. Linguistics arose in all the great written cultures of the past—in Babylon, in ancient Greece and Rome, in Hebrew and Arabic scholarship, in India, and in China—and the centrepiece of linguistics is a theory of grammar.

The grammar, of course, was a grammar of the written language. People were still unconscious of the nature of spontaneous conversation, and have remained so to this day; but they became aware of the structure of language through a study of what was written down. They became conscious of its principal constituent units, and gave names to them: first of all sentence and word, and later on phrase and clause. When punctuation developed, the boundary markers were associated with these grammatical units.

In spoken language, which has the same underlying grammar as written language, even though the two differ in certain very fundamental respects, there is always an association between grammatical units and prosodic ones. Thus, in English, there is a pattern whereby the clause (a grammatical unit) is associated with the tone group (a phonological unit, characterised by intonation: one melodic movement, or tone contour): other things being equal, each clause is spoken as one tone group. Hence, if one is writing connected discourse in English, the punctuation can be thought of (and is unconsciously interpreted) indifferently either as marking off grammatical units or as marking off prosodic units.

However, other things are often not equal. The reason why the association between clause and tone group is meaningful is precisely that it is **not** fixed, but varies systematically as a means of giving structure to the message. The tone group expresses a unit of information, what the speaker chooses to encode as a single message block; the relation of this to the clause is merely the base line, to which all other alignments can be related as a point of reference. So a speaker may organise a particular clause as two information units, or three; or combine two clauses into one. These are highlighted in the discourse because they are significant alternatives, each with its own particular meaning in the context.

What are the consequences for punctuation? If the writer is composing text in the written mode, the punctuation will simply follow the grammar; there is no implication of utterance, hence no prosody, no alternative pattern of organisation. But if the writer is composing with his ear, writing down what to him is essentially spoken discourse, then there is an implication of utterance; he is structuring the text prosodically as he goes along, and hence a conflict may arise. Is he to punctuate grammatically, or is he to punctuate phonologically? What is the basic unit through which he is working: the clause, or the tone group?

two styles of punctuation: according to the grammar, and according to the phonology

It is this alternative that lies behind many of the instances where we feel uncertain, or where in reading something we feel we would have punctuated it differently. There are two principles to choose from: punctuation according to grammar, and punctuation according to phonology. Much of the time it will make no difference: as long as clauses match up with tone groups, the two will come out the same. But where they differ, the two possibilities arise. Many writers shift between one and the other, or combine both if they can; but occasionally we come across a writer who seems strongly to favour one or the other type— who is at heart a grammatical punctuator, or a phonological punctuator; and then we see this as part of his or her individual style.

Here is an example of a sentence with different punctuations, showing the principles involved. A more detailed discussion of the tone group, and of the rhythm and intonation of spoken English, will be given below in Chapter 4.

Example of various punctuation

(a)	(b)
Freda leapt down from the gate, and as Sebastian came forward her look of recognition unmixed with any surprise, contrived to suggest that for her, the sudden appearance of someone who had been away for half her lifetime, was the most commonplace event imaginable.	Freda leapt down from the gate and, as Sebastian came forward, her look of recognition unmixed with any surprise contrived to suggest that, for her, the sudden appearance of someone who had been away for half her lifetime was the most commonplace event imaginable.

In version (b), the punctuation has followed the grammatical structure; but in version (a) it represents an interpretation of the text in phonological terms—each stretch between commas corresponding to a tone group. Note that in neither case does the comma imply a pause, although in loud reading it is often understood that way.

Written texts with minimal punctuation: punctuation and pausing

the minimum of punctuation: a legal document

There are registers in which punctuation is reduced to a minimum. The best known example is legal language: the old theory was that punctuation marks were too unstable to be relied on—they could be left out in copying, or fraudulently deleted or inserted; and so the ideal text was one that made use of no punctuation at all. Hence the production of sentences such as the following (from a mortgage agreement):

> That if the Mortgagor in the opinion of CAGA which opinion may be evidenced by a certificate under the hand of any one of the Attorneys referred to in Clause 45 of this Mortgage at any time makes default in duly performing or observing any of the convenants conditions or agreements on the part of the Mortgagor herein or in any security collateral hereto contained referred to or implied or any of the acts which ought to be performed according to any such covenants conditions or agreements it shall be lawful for but not obligatory upon CAGA without prejudice to any other right power or remedy of CAGA to perform or observe any such covenants conditions or agreements and for that purpose to do or attempt to do all such acts and things and to remedy or attempt to remedy any and every such default to the satisfaction of CAGA And all moneys so paid shall be repayable by the Mortgagor upon demand and be deemed part of the moneys secured hereby or in any security collateral hereto and carry interest accordingly until payment.
>
> (from CAGA *Memorandum of Mortgage*)

If we try to read this aloud, we are likely to end up breathless, because we have not taken time off to breathe. Punctuation provides a breathing space. Since texts of this kind are not meant to be read aloud, or even to be read at all—they are documentary records, written to be filed, and cited in evidence if the need arises—this has no real consequence one way or another.

In other kinds of text, the effect of 'hurrying the reader along' that is created by the absence of sentence-internal punctuation is a positive feature that may reflect an intention, conscious or unconscious, on the part of the writer. The following are two sentences taken from a maths textbook; note how the absence of punctuation seems to promote rapid reading, since there is no indication where internal boundaries should occur:

> Take a piece of wood about 25 cm long with one edge a straight edge and fix the semi-circle to the wood so that the diameter is along the straight edge. A piece of string about 10 cm long has one end attached to the centre of the diameter and a small weight to the other so that it may hang freely.
>
> (A. McMullen & J.L. Williams, *On Course Mathematics 2*, new edition, p.361)

The effect on reading aloud is very different if we rewrite it with internal boundaries.

> Take a piece of wood, about 25 cm long, with one edge a straight edge; and fix the semi-circle to the wood, so that the diameter is along the straight edge. A piece of string about 10 cm long has one end attached to the centre of the diameter, and a small weight to the other, so that it may hang freely.

Although in reading aloud we tend to insert pauses at the boundaries marked by punctuation, the pause itself is not a structural feature. If you listen to spontaneous discourse, there will of course be pauses from time to time; but not only are they fewer, and shorter, than those that are characteristic of loud-reading—they do not come in the same places. In natural speech pauses are not, on the whole, associated with grammatical boundaries; rather, the speaker tends to pause in the middle of a structure when he or she comes to an unexpected word (one that has a low frequency in the language, or is not predictable from the context). This can be thought of as time spent searching for the word in question, or as consideration for the listener; but it is of course quite unconscious.

There is very rarely any pause, however, at grammatical or phonological boundaries. The 'boundary' between one clause and another is an analytic concept; while that between one tone group and another is a complex melodic and rhythmic phenomenon, mainly signalled by a change in the contour of the melody and not located at any exact point in time. In neither case is there any determinable period of silence; the pause, if it does occur, is merely an optional extra. Hence what the punctuation is actually representing, whether grammatical or phonological in its orientation, is not any kind of pausing. If we pause when reading aloud, this is a special feature associated with that activity, where written text is being consciously reprocessed and translated into the spoken medium.

Functions of the written language

Writing evolves in response to needs that arise as a result of cultural changes. The particular circumstance that led to the development of writing was the complex of events whereby certain human groups changed over from a mobile way of life to permanent settlement: from a predominantly hunting and gathering economy to a predominantly agricultural one.

People in hunting and gathering communities tend to live in small, highly mobile groups; their social structure is complex, but neither the functioning of their social institutions nor the transmission of their cultural knowledge would gain any advantage from writing. The spoken language serves their requirements perfectly adequately; indeed, that is precisely what it evolved in order to do.

When some communities took to husbanding and cultivating, and so ensuring a regular and increasing supply of food, their patterns of culture underwent certain fundamental changes: populations increased, there was 'division of labour', power structures arose, wealth was distributed and inherited, and goods and services were controlled and exchanged. In certain areas, such as the great river valleys of Egypt, south and south-west Asia, and northern China, permanently settled agricultural communities developed highly complex cultural institutions for whose purposes the spoken language was no longer enough. Language had to be reduced to a form where it **existed** rather than simply **happening**—where a text could be referred to over and over again, instead of having to be performed each time like the literature and sacred texts of oral communities. In modern jargon, a **process** had to be transformed into a **product**.

Writing evolves to serve new functions of language in society.

There was, as we have seen, a resource ready to hand: people had been making visual images for tens or hundreds of generations, so it was natural to exploit this ability and map the visual representations on to language. This enabled language to satisfy a new range of functional demands. Writing was used for marking and inventorying property, for invoicing goods being traded, for collecting taxes, for recording tribute received; it was used for astronomical and calendrical records, for codifying the laws, and for keeping accurate measurements of land. But once it had come into existence, it also took over some functions that had previously been fulfilled by spoken language: religious, literary, and oratorical. Sacred texts, lyric and epic poetry, and panegyrics began to be written down, and then came to be composed in writing; exploits were celebrated and philosophical positions argued out through the composition of written texts. And writing took over the main burden of the transmission of cultural knowledge: 'education' came into being.

This is not the place to attempt a general interpretation of oral and literate cultures. There are several very penetrating studies that have become (or will become) classics: for example, the work of Marshall McLuhan, Jack Goody, and Walter Ong (McLuhan 1962; Goody 1968; Ong 1982). Here we need to say something more briefly about the functions of writing in our own society, and then move on to a consideration of written language.

We are so surrounded by written language that we can hardly conceive of life without it. Because it is so pervasive we are inclined to take for granted that everybody is using written language all the time, rather than actually inquiring into what people achieve through reading and writing. Yet there are illiterate members within our society: most children under five, and an appreciable number of adults—the number will depend on how we decide to set our criteria, but is likely to fall somewhere between 5 and 20 per cent. What do they lose by being illiterate?

the place of written language in our everyday lives

As adults, we read for action (and interaction), for information, and for entertainment. It is instructive to keep a 'language diary' from time to time, and record all that one has read during the course of a week. The final list might look something like the following:

1. **primarily for action**
   public signs, e.g. on roads and stations; product labels and instructions, e.g. on food, tools, or toys purchased; recipes; maps; television and radio guides; bills; menus; telephone directories; ballot papers; computer manuals, monitors, and printouts
   for social contact
   personal correspondence: letters, postcards, greeting cards
2. **primarily for information**
   newspapers (news, editorials) and current affairs magazines; hobby magazines; non-fiction books, including textbooks; public notices; advertisements; political pamphlets; scholastic, medical, etc. reports; guidebooks and travel literature

3. **primarily for entertainment**
   light magazines, comic strips; fiction books; poetry and drama; newspaper features; film subtitles; games, including computer games.

The categories are not clear cut; what is for information now may be for action later, what is instructional may also have entertainment value, and so on. But this gives a fair sample of what a literate adult can expect to achieve through reading. One important variable, of course, is the amount and kind of reading that is involved in his or her professional activities.

What about writing? It is said that many highly educated people, including many teachers, actually write very little, and this may be so. No doubt for a considerable section of every community the main environment for writing throughout their lives has been the school. But the picture has probably been oversimplified. For one thing, it is not clear exactly what is to count as writing. If someone is using a typewriter, he is presumably 'writing' within the sense that matters; but what about if he is dictating a letter to his secretary, or into a machine, or entering a program into a computer? It may be that 'writing' has been defined rather narrowly, as written composition in certain specific registers; or as 'putting pen to paper', which is certainly something many people rarely do except when signing their names.

Whether you write or not, once you are functionally literate in a literate society, you are in fact participating in the exchange of meanings through written language; and this has considerable significance, since the kinds of meaning that are transmitted in writing tend to be somewhat different from the kinds of meaning transmitted through speech.

Forms of written English

Written language never was, and never has been, conversation written down. It is only very recently, since the invention of the tape recorder, that we have been able to make written transcriptions of natural spontaneous speech; and it is very clear that they are not what writing is about. The main purpose of writing down speech, in fact, is to enable us to study speech; it is certainly not to provide a model of what written language ought to look like.

Written language, and written texts, take on a higher value in the culture.

The boot, in fact, has usually been worn on the other foot. In literate communities it is writing, rather than speech, that is highly valued; and if people argue that speech and writing should resemble each other it is usually because they would like you to speak as you write, rather than to write as you speak. At the same time, they usually recognise that the process should not go too far: it may be thought desirable to speak with the clarity and accuracy that are ascribed to written language, but not to 'talk like a book'.

At various times, in the history of various cultures, spoken and written language have moved very far apart, sometimes to the extent of being entirely different languages. Thus in medieval Europe people spoke English, French, Italian, Dutch, and so on; but almost everything they wrote was in Latin. In China until 1919 most writing was

the variable distance between spoken and written varieties of a language; 'diglossia' one form of outcome in classical Chinese—which although it was called by the same name (by the Chinese themselves) was by that time about as far from spoken Chinese as Latin is from French; and there is a similar distance in most of the Arabic-speaking communities between classical and spoken Arabic. This situation, referred to in linguistics as DIGLOSSIA, is characteristic of certain social conditions, where a 'high' variety of language is maintained for certain prestigious functions, alongside the 'low' varieties or vernaculars.

In such conditions, the two do not readily mix (except perhaps for comic purposes, like the student songs of medieval Europe in which Latin was mixed with the vernacular). At other times, however, spoken and written language are not so far apart. They represent different registers within a single language, and, as such, are not clearly defined categories but rather clusterings of particular tendencies (tendencies that we shall be studying in the next two chapters). This allows for all kinds of intermediate and approximating varieties, where other factors come into play to determine the forms the language takes: level of formality, topic under discussion, and so on.

To exemplify the varieties of written English that would be typically associated with the functions outlined in the previous section, one might assemble an anthology of specimens of each of the following:

a road sign	a light magazine
a product label	a comic strip
a map	a short story
a recipe	a novel
a graffito	a play
a set of instructions	a poem
a bill	an essay
a menu	a review
a television guide	a letter to the press
a telephone directory	
a ballot paper	a dictionary entry
a computer manual	a will
	an agreement
a personal letter	a subtitle
a newsreport	
an editorial	
a current affairs article	
a hobby magazine	
a text book	
an advertisement	
a public notice	
a political pamphlet	
a sports report	
a travel brochure	

Variation and written language

the difference between 'writing' and 'written language'

It is important to distinguish, therefore, between WRITING, in the sense of a system of writing—the symbols and their functions in the

42

language—and WRITTEN LANGUAGE, what is produced in the written medium.

The writing system is the means whereby the meanings engendered by the particular language are 'put out' (expressed) in visual instead of spoken form. As we saw, this is achieved by a set of symbols having conventional values for representing the wordings of the language, either singly or in combination; with principles for creating new combinations when needed. The individual symbols may refer either to lexicogrammatical elements, as in Chinese, or to phonological elements, as in English. Figure 3.2 gives a diagrammatic representation of this.

Figure 3.2 How writing systems represent language

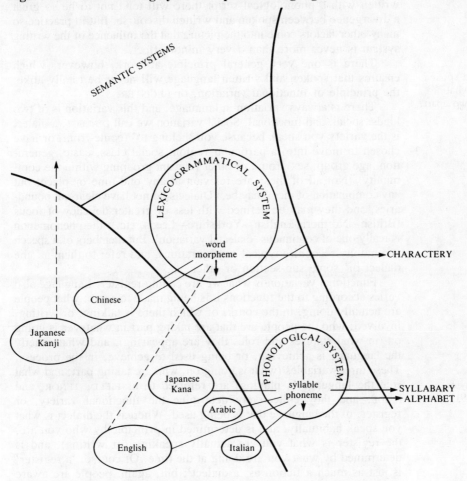

The written language is the functional variety of the language that is typically used in texts that are composed in writing. It is, obviously, a kind of English (or Chinese, or whatever), not some altogether distinct language; but it displays lexico-grammatical and semantic characteristics that differ in certain respects from the characteristics of spoken language (spoken English, spoken Chinese, etc.). We shall be investigating these differences in the next two chapters.

The nature of the writing system has some effect on the nature of the written language; but not very much. For example, because Chinese is written with a charactery, in which each morpheme has its own symbol and no matter how many morphemes are pronounced alike they will always be written differently, it is possible for the written language to diverge very considerably from the spoken form, which it often tends to do. There is no requirement that what is written should be intelligible when read aloud. With a phonological writing system, on the other hand, if a text is unintelligible when read aloud, it will also be unintelligible in writing, since the writing merely symbolises the spoken expression (and, as we have seen, it leaves out some of that). Hence in languages written with a phonological script there will tend not to be so great a divergence between spoken and written discourse. But in practice so many other factors come into the picture that the influence of the writing system is never more than a very minor effect.

There is one very general principle at work, however, which ensures that spoken and written language will never be totally alike: the principle of functional variation, or REGISTER.

Written and spoken language: what keeps the two apart?

There is always variation in language; and this variation is of two kinds: social, and functional. Social variation we call DIALECT: a dialect is the variety you speak because you 'belong to' (come from, or have chosen to move into) a particular region, social class, caste, generation, age group, sex group, or other relevant grouping within the community. (Not all of these are relevant at any one time or place; but any combination of them may be.) Dialects do not have clear-cut boundaries, and they may be defined with less or greater delicacy of focus (British—Northern English—Yorkshire—Leeds, etc.); the phenomenon is really one of continuous 'dialectal variation'. But members of a speech community recognise typical configurations, and refer to them as 'the dialect of' some sub-section or other.

Functional variation is what we are calling register. Language also varies according to the functions it is being made to serve: what people are actually doing, in the course of which there is talking, or writing, involved; who the people are that are taking part in whatever is going on (in what statuses and roles they are appearing); and what exactly the language is achieving, or being used to achieve, in the process. These three variables (what is going on; who are taking part; and what role the language is playing) are referred to as FIELD, TENOR, and MODE; and they collectively determine the functional variety, or register, of the language that is being used. Whereas the dialect is what you speak habitually, and is determined in principle by who you are, the register is what you are actually speaking (or writing), and is determined by what you are doing at the time. Of course, 'a register' is just as much a fiction as 'a dialect'; but, again, people are aware that language varies in this way, and talk readily about 'the language of poetry', 'the language of the law', and so on. There was however no separate term for 'functional variety', so the term 'register' was introduced for it in linguistics.

See Halliday & Hasan (1989).

Now writing evolved for a range of distinct social functions; it was not primarily a new way of doing old things with language. In other words it came into being precisely so that **new** registers could be created: so that there could be a 'written language' that was not the same as

44

the spoken. Again, this is not to imply that there will be one clearly defined 'written' variety; what emerges is a new range of functional variation, which leads to the emergence of configurations of semantic and lexico-grammatical patterns that then come to be recognised as characteristic of writing. One can see this process happening straight away in languages that have just recently come to be written down—for example, a number of Australian Aboriginal languages, which immediately start to develop their own written forms. And there is nothing surprising about this, when we remember that there was already register variation in the spoken language before writing ever came on the scene. Unwritten languages also vary in register: there are differences among casual conversation, traditional narrative, religious discourse, instructional discourse, poetry, 'mother-in-law' language, and so on. Written language adds a new dimension to the variation, because of the new functions it serves; but the principle of such variation has always been there.

the emergence of written registers

All these varieties can of course influence each other, and in a literate community there is 'feedback' from writing into speech, particularly because of the prestige with which written registers tend to be endowed. We will say something about that in the final chapter. Meanwhile in the next chapter we take up the topic of characteristics of spoken English.

Chapter 4

Spoken language: prosodic features

Speech and transcription

Although we use the term 'written language', this does not mean that there is one invariant type of English that is associated with all forms of written discourse. There is a whole cluster of different varieties—a scatter of types of variation—that share the written medium. But we can refer to certain features of the language as being characteristic of written registers; and if we talk about somebody using the 'written mode', this is an informal way of suggesting that the language used is that of a text that would typically be found in writing.

In the same way, we refer to 'spoken language', again without implying that all forms of speech are alike. But there are features characteristic of spoken registers just as there are of written; and in similar fashion we can talk about the 'spoken mode'.

If we want to bring out the essential differences between spoken and written language, we can best do this by the strategy of selecting a kind of paradigm case and treating it as representative of the category. For spoken language, then, we shall take natural spontaneous conversation as the paradigm form. In its 'ideal' form, this means dialogue; but we shall not need to insist on the distinction between dialogue and monologue, because a great deal of spontaneous conversation has a large amount of monologue embedded in it.

Here are two short passages of what we would recognise as natural conversation:

(recorded by Elaine Daisley)

A: How's Fred going with his pacemaker in his heart?
B: Oh, he's all right.
C: He's all right.
B: He's younger now.
D: Running around; betting like anything.
A: Is he?
D: Cranky as ever.
E: Cranky he is, Alice.
A: Yes.
E: The horse don't win, it's the jockey that's pulled it up, or something—or some other thing.

spontaneous conversation as the characteristic form of spoken language

46

C: It's all right when it wins though. He only goes crook when they lose.

D: It was funny today. I had this horse, Alice, and —

E: And what did you get for your double?

D: But wait till I tell you about this horse. Cause I can't see much, you know, and I said to Doris, 'Oh,' I said, 'I may as well have a double, I suppose,' so we're just picking them out and trying to fossick them out, you know, so I put the extra double and I had about three with those other horses—about four, and —

C: Number one won it.

D: Oh yes; number one won the first, extra leg, and . . . yeah, number one.

C: Mum said 'Oh, I haven't got that.'

D: I said 'Oh, I haven't got it.' And then — they protested; and my horse won it by protesting. And then the second one got up and it paid seventy odd dollars.

A: Oh my goodness.

C: And she was going crook. She says —

F: So you got seventy odd dollars today.

D: I got about eighty-two altogether.

F: Today.

D: Today. A good day's work.

(recorded by Pamela Riley)

A: Actually there's one argument that goes—this is not in relation to the Hungarians; this is the Russians—that essentially the Russian peasants, agricultural labourers, were better off under the Tsarists than they have been under the Stalinist regime; that, you know, their real income, real peasant income, has declined under the —

B: I thought this was the kulaks.

A: Oh, no; the kulaks were rich peasants.

B: Yes, that's right; they were the ones that ruled others.

A: These were the serfs, essentially; the serfs, the labouring people. The real income of the serfs had declined; and actually this is an argument that many—that the anti-Soviet Marxists use too: they say that what's happened is that Russia exploited the peasants—that the Stalinist regime exploited the peasants to pay for, you know, to fund their industrialisation.

B: Yes, I think that's so too.

A: Whereas this is the criticism that the Chinese make of them: they say they're —

B: I think that's probably true; I mean, I think that if you're going to change a whole society you're going to have to have very . . . you know, someone's going to suffer and there are going to be —

C: Like, everyone?

B: Well, you know, you could say the Chinese landlords, or whatever, suffered at the Chinese regime; but for the majority life improved, and there's no-one who could possibly deny that.

C: Life improved in the west at the same time; don't forget that.

B: Oh yes, I'm not—the west: you know, I'm not really bringing that into it, but—

A: That's actually one of the points that Galbraith has made, you know: that whatever you say about capitalism—this is something of course that Marx says about capitalism—it relieved — it released the mass of the people from what he called the idiocy of rural life.

Here they have been transcribed into ordinary written English, with consequent loss of a certain amount of the meaning. There are alternative ways of transcribing that incorporate different facets of what the writing system leaves out. There is no way of incorporating every last detail; and certainly no point in trying, since the transcription soon becomes so cluttered as to be unreadable. What one has to do is decide which features are important for the purpose in hand, and leave the others out.

We shall adopt a particular form for the transcription of conversational text, designed to incorporate the features that will be described in this present chapter. A brief reference will be made to other methods of transcription in current use.

Mention was made earlier of the 'language diary', the idea of keeping a record of language use. This can give interesting results with spoken language, if one makes notes on the various patterns of speech that have accompanied one's verbal encounters in the course of a day. It can also be a useful technique in teaching, since pupils over a wide age range can become aware of spoken language in this way.

Intonation and rhythm

All natural speech, in any language, is marked by patterns of intonation and rhythm—what Joshua Steele, who first described them in detail (1775), called the 'melody and measure of speech'. Intonation is the melodic movement, the rise and fall in pitch. Rhythm is the 'beat' of the language, which gives it an organisation in time. Both are prosodic features: they are part of the system of the language.

The **particular** function of intonation and rhythm, the contribution they make to discourse, will vary from one language to another, although there are certain general tendencies that apply to all. As a general rule, the function of rhythm is internal to the phonological system: that is, it imposes organisation on the sound of language, particularly the patterning of the syllables, but does not by itself express contrasts in meaning.

tone and intonation; tone languages; intonation as the expression of grammatical distinctions

Intonation, on the other hand, functions in the lexico-grammatical system: it encodes some aspect of the wording, and therefore directly expresses contrasts in meaning.

In some languages, intonation has a lexical function: the choice of TONE (say, falling as opposed to level or rising) is as much part of the phonetic shape of a word as is the choice of vowels and consonants, so that if you vary the tone you get a different word. These languages are called TONE LANGUAGES: well-known examples are Chinese, Vietnamese, and Thai. In other languages, it has a grammatical function: the choice of INTONATION (the pitch contour of a clause or phrase) expresses some aspect of the speech function, usually having something to do with certainty or doubt; and the LOCATION OF PITCH PROMINENCE (where the main fall or rise in pitch occurs) often carries some information about how the discourse is organised into messages, and what the listener is expected to attend to.

Probably in all languages there is **some** use of intonation as a grammatical feature; but less in tone languages, for obvious reasons (since pitch variation is already doing something else)—it is minimal in Vietnamese and Cantonese. English is at the other end of the scale; it is not a tone language, and it makes a great deal of use of intonation to carry grammatical meaning.

It may seem strange to refer to the function of intonation as grammatical; but there are good reasons for doing so. In the first place, the contrasts expressed by intonation are quite systematic, like other contrasts in the grammar; they are not vague and individualistic nuances. Secondly, they are closely tied to other grammatical systems, such as mood and modality; it is impossible to describe these systems in detail **without** taking account of intonation. Thirdly, since intonation can express lexical meaning (that is, can function as part of the shape of a word, as it does in a tone language), it is only to be expected that it will also be able to function in the grammar. This is not to say that descriptions of intonation in terms like 'excited' or 'doubtful' are wrong; merely that, if such terms are used, they **become** grammatical terms and need to be understood as systematically related both to each other, and to other grammatical categories.

In the next three sections we will give a short account of the rhythm and intonation of spoken English.

English rhythm

In a line of verse, we can hear the rhythm clearly. It may be determined by the METRE, the particular verse form that is chosen, as in

> I passed by his garden, and marked, with one eye,
> How the Owl and the Panther were sharing a pie.
> (L. Carroll, *Through the Looking Glass*, ch.10)

Here it is clear that the beat falls on the following syllables: *passed*, *gar* (in *garden*), *marked*, *eye*, *owl*, *pan* (in *panther*), *shar* (in *sharing*), and *pie*. These syllables are STRONG; the others are WEAK. We will express this by the following notation, using a slash / analogously to the bar line in music—that is, immediately before the beat:

> I / passed by his / garden and / marked with one / eye how the
> / Owl and the / Panther were / sharing a / pie

Frequently, however, the rhythm of verse is not determined by the metre; the metre is an idealised pattern that lies behind the poem overall, whereas the rhythm is the actual value with which the lines are invested

rhythm in language;
rhythm and metre

(and may be varied, of course, from one reading to another). So if we take Browning's line *Hours and long hours in the dead night, I ask* the metre, which is iambic pentameter, would put the stress on every second word: *and*, *hours*, *the*, *night*, *ask*:

As here I lie
In this state-chamber, dying by degrees,
Hours and long hours in the dead night, I ask
'Do I live? Am I dead?' Peace, peace seems all.
Saint Praxed's ever was the church for peace.
(Robert Browning: 'The Bishop orders his tomb at Saint Praxed's Church')

Rhythmically, however, a probable reading of the line would be:

/ hours and / long / hours in the / dead / night I / ask

which is how it would sound as a segment of natural speech.

Natural discourse in English is rhythmic in just this way. Here is an example from the speech of a six-year-old, who asked 'Why are there more floods in houses in the basement? I should have thought the roof was more likely to leak than the ground floor'. Rhythmically:

/ why are there / more / floods in / houses in the / basement /

the foot as the unit
of rhythm in spoken
English

Notice that the number of syllables from one beat to the next can vary, just like the number of notes in a musical bar. The 'bar' in language is referred to as a FOOT, following the terminology of metrics—in some ways a bad choice of term, because the rhythmic foot is not the same thing as the metric foot, but we will continue to use it here. Note that the (rhythmic) foot always begins with the beat (unlike the metric foot, but, again, like the bar).

Let us indicate the number of syllables in each foot, in the above example:

/ why are there /	more /	floods in /	houses in the /	basement /
3	1	2	4	2

In some languages, such as French and Hindi, the basic unit of rhythm is the syllable: all **syllables** are more or less the same length. In other languages, the basic unit of rhythm is the foot. English is a 'foot-timed' language (sometimes called 'stress-timed', because the syllable carrying the beat is strong, or 'stressed'). In English, all **feet** are more or less the same length.

The key words in both cases are 'more or less'. If speech maintained strict tempo, then the feet would be **exactly** the same length; which would mean that in a foot with four syllables each syllable would be only one quarter the length of a syllable that occurred in a foot all by itself. This does happen in some contexts; for example, reciting a list like the months of the year (see Figure 4.1).

But in ordinary conversation the timing is not so exact. A two-syllable foot tends to be a little bit longer than a one-syllable one, but nothing like twice as long—whereas if the language was timed by the syllable, two syllables would take twice as long as one. The typical proportion is roughly as in Table 4.1.

Figure 4.1   Recitation of the months

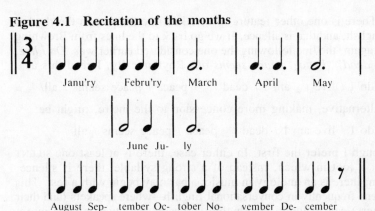

Note: *January* and *February* have alternative readings in 4/4 time; but if this is used the tempo changes to triple time half-way through the list.

Table 4.1   Relative duration of feet having different numbers of syllables

example   / why are there / more / floods in / houses in the / basement /

no of syllables in foot:	3	1	2	4	2
proportionate duration:	1.4	1	1.2	1.6	1.2

In other words, taking a one-syllable foot as having a duration of 1 unit, then a two-syllable foot will average 1.2 units; i.e. it will be one fifth as long again. A three-syllable foot will average 1.4; and so on. The tempo of speech varies considerably, of course; but something like half a second is a fairly typical duration for a one-syllable foot in not too rapid conversation. Hence the actual timing for this utterance might have been something like that in Table 4.2.

the relative length of different feet, and therefore of syllables within the foot

Table 4.2   Typical duration of feet (in seconds)

	/ why are there / more / floods in / houses in the / basement /
seconds:	0.7 0.5 0.6 0.8 0.6

This means that English syllables get contracted or expanded according to the arrangement of strong and weak: all syllables have to fit in the rhythmic pattern set by the strong ones (including the strong syllables themselves, since their length also has to accommodate).

Furthermore, the total time taken up by the foot is not always divided equally among its constituent syllables. The **relative** duration of syllables in the foot is also entirely systematic; it is determined by a combination of grammatical and phonological factors that is too complex to go into here, but that is very clearly described by Abercombie (1965) in the chapters dealing with rhythm (*Studies in Phonetics and Linguistics*, Chapters 3–5). These facts are important for anyone interested in the relation between conversational rhythm and the rhythm of poetry.

There is one other feature to be taken into account in the rhythm of English, and that is silence. If we go back to the lines from Browning once again, the line following the one considered earlier was *'Do I live, am I dead?' Peace, peace seems all*. Rhythmically, I read this as

. . . do I / live / ˎ am I / dead / ˎ / peace / peace seems / all/

An alternative, making more concession to the metre, might be:

. . . do I / live am I / dead / ˎ peace / peace seems / all /

the silent beat
—though I prefer the first. In either case, there is at least one SILENT BEAT: a foot in which, instead of a strong syllable, there is silence. Again, there is an anology in music: a bar may begin with a rest. This happens frequently in conversational English—where speakers (and their listeners) can maintain the rhythm across at least two, maybe more, 'feet' consisting entirely of silence.

Coming back to our conversational example, there was a silent beat between the two parts:

/ why are there / more / floods in / houses in the / basement / ˎ
I should have / thought the / roof was more / likely to / leak than the / ground / floor /

This silent beat can be an important structural signal: it helps, along with the intonation, to show the distinction between a non-defining and a defining relative clause:

/ people who / live in / glass / houses . . . (defining)
/ eskimos / ˎ who / live in / ice / houses . . . (non-defining)

The writing system signals the possibility of a silent beat by means of a comma: *people who live in glass houses . . .* versus *Eskimos, who live in ice houses, . . .*

Conventionally, we will show an utterance which starts with one or more weak syllables as having a silent beat at the beginning:

/ ˎ do I / live / ˎ am I / dead . . .

One of the main problems faced by foreign learners of English is getting the rhythm right—especially if their own language is predominantly syllable-timed, and does not contain weak or reduced syllables. But rhythm can be one of the main reasons for not being understood by English speakers. Practice in strict tempo rhythm with feet of different length is an effective way of rapidly improving the level of intelligibility.

the particularly rhythmic quality of spontaneous conversation
All forms of spoken English are rhythmic; but the more unconscious the speech the more rhythmic it is likely to be. Reading aloud a prepared text (unless it is overtly rhythmic in its form), or talking in a situation where one has to monitor oneself (in a formal context, or on a difficult topic), tends to detract from the regularity of the rhythm. Spontaneous conversation of a natural, unselfconscious kind is usually the most rhythmically patterned of all.

English intonation: tonicity and tone

Rhythm is closely linked to intonation, since it is the strong syllables that carry the burden of the melody.

The foot, in itself, is not a unit of meaning. It does not express any semantic structure. **Which** syllables are strong in any instance is fixed within limits determined by the wording; essentially, the principle is that:

1. Words of more than one syllable have an ACCENT on a particular syllable; the accented syllable is strong, others are weak. Long words may have more than one accent.
2. Words of one syllable are (a) strong, if lexical ('content' words), (b) weak, if grammatical ('function' words).
3. Any word, and any syllable of any word, can be strong for special prominence or contrast.

But there is a phonological unit that is larger than the foot, and that is the unit of intonation, known as the TONE GROUP. The tone group does represent a meaningful segment of the discourse. Each tone group is, so to speak, one quantum of the message, the way the speaker is organising it as he goes along.

We will mark the boundary of the tone group with a double slash, making it (by convention) always coincide with a foot boundary. The **exact** location of the boundary is indeterminate, since one tone group mellows without pause into another; but we can, in fact, identify it to the nearest foot, which is all that matters.

A tone group has two significant properties. One is that it contains a particular point of prominence, referred to as the TONIC, or TONIC NUCLEUS; this property we refer to as its TONICITY. The other is that it selects one of a small number of melodic contours or TONES; this property we shall simply call its TONE. The melody may have one part to it or two: that is, it consists either **just** of a TONIC SEGMENT (the part that contains the tonic nucleus), or of a tonic sement **preceded** by another, PRETONIC SEGMENT.

the tone group as the unit of intonation in spoken English; tonicity and tone

We will mark the tonic nucleus by **bold type** (wavy underlining in manuscript or typescript). It is always located at one particular foot, where it is the word containing the strong syllable that carries the prominence. Let us exemplify from the same piece of text as before:

// why are there / more / floods in / houses in the / **basement** //

Here the tonic is at the end, on the word *basement*. The second sentence, however, contains two tone groups, with tonic prominence on *roof* and again on *ground*:

// I should have / thought the / **roof** was more / likely to / leak than the // **ground** / floor //

We will mark the tone in two ways (it does no harm to introduce a little redundancy into the transcription): (1) by a number at the beginning of the tone group, after the double slash, and (2) by a diacritical symbol inserted above the tonic syllable. The set of tones—number, description, and diacritic—is as follows:

tone 1	fall \	
tone 2	rise /	(or 2 sharp fall-rise V)
tone 3	low rise ⌐	
tone 4	fall-rise ∨	
tone 5	rise-fall ∧	

tone 13   fall + low rise \ ⌣
tone 53   rise-fall + low rise ∧⌣

Tones 'one-three' and 'five-three' are, as they appear, combinations of two of the five basic tones; but they occur on a single tone group—which therefore has two tonic nuclei instead of just one.

We can now transcribe the example in its final form:

//1 why are there / more / floods in / houses in the / **bàsement** //1 ˌI should have / thought the / **roòf** was more / likely to / leak than the // 4 **ground** / floor //

It will be helpful at this point to depict the entire contour, so as to make clear the relation between the tone and tonicity (see Figure 4.2).

Figure 4.2   Intonation contour

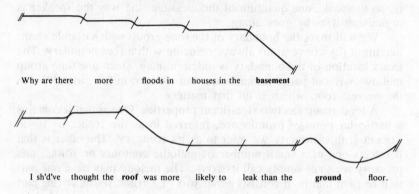

Why are there   more   floods in   houses in the   **basement**

I sh'd've   thought the **roof** was more   likely to   leak than the   **ground**   floor.

patterns of pitch
movement in speech:
the intonation
contour

What this figure shows is that while the information contour is a continuous flow, with some stepping up and stepping down, there is in each tone group one place where the pitch changes dramatically—where the roller-coaster suddenly dips or rises, or does both one after the other.

That increased pitch **movement**, the place where the pitch is at its most dynamic, is the point of prominence in the tone group. It can be clearly heard, once one has learnt to attend to it—this takes a little bit of practice, with a tape repeater loop or transcribing machine; but **unconsciously**, of course, we hear it every time. Acoustically, it is a complex phenomenon comprising features of pitch, length, and loudness (i.e. fundamental frequency, duration, and intensity); but the key factor is pitch change. The tonic syllable is often slightly longer than its place in the rhythm would determine; and it may also be marginally louder, though this is the least important factor in its identification.

The meaning of tonic prominence

What is the semantic function of tonicity? Let us go back to the notion of the INFORMATION UNIT: what the speaker chooses to present as one portion of message. This is what the tone group is for: one tone group is the expression of one unit of information.

Information in the linguistic sense is not the same thing as information in mathematics, although it is not totally unrelated to it. Infor-

54

mation is a property of connected discourse, involving the interaction of two complementary parts: what is 'given', and what is 'new'. 'Given' means known, or at least knowable, to the listener at this point in the discourse; 'new' means unknown, or non-recoverable. In principle, an information unit is a balanced construction of the given and the new.

But information is, of course, in the gift of the speaker. It is not some objectifiable commodity. In analysing discourse into its given and new elements, one can usually point to factors of the context (context of situation, and preceding text) that have determined what is given and is new; but in the last resort it is the speaker's decision what is to be **treated** as one or the other. So the 'new' is really 'what I (the speaker) tell you (the listener) to **attend** to'—what you're being offered as news. The 'given' constitutes the ground against which this news is made to figure.

The tone group as information unit; information consists of what is 'given' and what is 'new'.

Tonic prominence marks the **culmination** of what is new in the particular information unit. Anything **after** the tonic, but still in the same tone group, is thereby signalled as given; for example, *more likely to leak* in the current fragment. What comes **before** the tonic may be all new, or may start with something given; so that the total formula for the information unit is (G) N (G)—obligatory New element, optionally preceded and/or followed by something Given.

But there is an UNMARKED pattern, which has the New at the end: (G) N. Other things being equal, the new element comes last in the information unit, and anything that is given precedes it. This is extremely important for the written language, because it means that in writing one normally organises matters so that each clause proceeds from Given to New, on the assumption of two related unmarked options ('default' choices):

1. that each RANKING (i.e. non-EMBEDDED) clause is one information unit; and
2. that in each information unit, what is given (if anything) precedes what is new

— so that a reader can assume (1) that each ranking clause is one tone group and (2) that in each tone group the tonic comes at the end. We shall see in Chapter 5 that there are certain clause structures that signal the occurrence of other, MARKED distributions.

The unmarked pattern is the one that is likely to figure in the opening passage of a discourse, since there is usually no good reason for choosing anything else. So Nigel, in this example, begins with an information unit in which everything is New—he is just introducing the subject, out of the blue—so the tonic comes at the end, on *basement*. In the second part, however, he introduces two marked features: the clause is structured into two information units, to mark the contrast between *roof* and *ground* (*floor*); and each of these has a marked information structure, with given material following after the new. In the first, *more likely to leak* is treated as given, since the preceding clause has already introduced the topic of *floods in houses*; while in the second, the tonic is on *ground*, leaving *floor* as given because it is implicit in basement (and perhaps also *roof*).

the dynamic of natural speech; marked and unmarked patterns of given and new information

Thus there is a dynamic quality in spoken discourse whereby the pattern of information flow is a sequence of small crescendos, each one being a movement from a less prominent, more predictable onset towards a more prominent, less predictable climax. That represents the base line, as it were.

But if that pattern was maintained invariant over a long stretch, its effectiveness would be diminished; there is an inherent contradiction involved in creating a structure for organising the unpredictable. There has to **be** a structure, otherwise no meaning can be construed by departing from it; but by the same token, there has to be an interplay between the departure and the norm. Hence whereas in written language there is a tendency to proceed lineally from the known to the informative (since there is no resource in the writing system for expressing this kind of meaning), in spoken language there is a great deal of variation, as the speakers exploit the potential of tonicity to its full rhetorical effect.

The meaning of tone

It has been known for a long time that the rise and fall in the pitch of the voice was meaningful. Its place in English grammar was pointed out a hundred years ago by the distinguished grammarian Henry Sweet (1898).

Although tone languages make use of the contrast between high and low (**static** pitch features can serve for lexical distinctions), intonation systems always use pitch **dynamically**. The fundamental opposition used for grammatical purposes is not that between high and low, but that between falling and rising.

Children master this opposition very early, well before they control the mechanisms of articulation; and it seems to have a near-universal significance, in that falling pitch is in some way associated with satisfaction and rising pitch with 'something needs to be done'. The second of these, in early childhood, usually means a request for action; but in the adult language a craving is a craving for information, so here rising pitch usually means a question. But the precise meaning varies considerably from one language to another.

the meaning of pitch variation: falling, rising, and level contours

In English, the particular significance of the falling tone is that of confidence about POLARITY—the speaker knows whether the point at issue is positive or negative. So tone 1 expresses a statement, as in *it's Tuesday*; and it also expresses a WH-question, as in *what day is it?*, where although the speaker is uncertain about something it is not a question of yes or no—he or she simply wants a missing piece supplied. Tone 2, on the other hand, expresses a yes/no question, as in *is it Tuesday?*: the rise in pitch signals 'polarity unknown'.

The third term in this opposition is neither falling or rising but, in principle, level—that is, it 'opts out' of the choice, suspending a decision so to speak. In practice it never is level, but always carries a slight rise, signalling 'message incomplete'. This tone is used to show an information unit that is dependent on another one: it might be an item in a list (other than the last), a statement that is going to be followed by 'and' plus another one co-ordinated to it, or a circumstantial expression, such as time or place, that is added at the end. The last—statement ending with circumstantial element—is the typical meaning of tone 13, a fall with a low rise attached to it, as in *There's some beer in the fridge.*

Before we go on to tones 4 and 5, there is an important point to be made. I have said 'tone 1 expresses a statement', 'tone 2 expresses a yes/no question', and so on; but the grammar will tell us that a statement is expressed by a DECLARATIVE clause, a question by an INTERROGATIVE. How do we reconcile these two assertions?

'The grammar' that we are referring to has always been a grammar of written English, where there are no tones; so there is no source of possible conflict. But clause classes—declarative, WH- interrogative, yes/no interrogative, imperative, and their numerous subcategories—**are** present in **spoken** English, where they can be just as clearly distinguished as in writing. So what is it that signals a statement in spoken English: is it the declarative mood, or the falling tone, or both together?

Since these categories do not always go together—you will hear declaratives on tone 2, and yes/no interrogatives on tone 1—it cannot be both. Yet the meanings are undeniably associated: **other things being equal,** they do go together. And that provides the answer: the clause class and the tone express different meanings, but meanings that are closely related so that there is an unmarked option to combine them in certain ways: typically, declarative and WH- interrogative clauses go with tone 1, and yes/no interrogative clauses go with tone 2.

It is important for this reason to keep the terms apart. Declarative, interrogative, and imperative are **grammatical** categories; the choice among them is called MOOD. Statement, question, and command are **semantic** categories: the choice is that of SPEECH FUNCTION. The semantic categories are actually expressed by a combination of mood and tone; but these categories would have to be considerably further refined if we wanted to present them in an integrated form and this would take us beyond our present scope. For this discussion therefore we will keep the two apart, and refer to the meaning of the choice of tone as KEY. This will enable us to talk about it separately from speech function.

speech function, mood, and 'key': the relation of intonation to telling, asking, ordering, etc.

To return to tones 4 and 5. These arose as combinations of the basic movements, and this is clearly reflected in their meaning. Tone 4, the fall-rise, has a sense of 'it may seem cut and dried, but it isn't'; so it is a tone of reservation and contrast—there is a 'but' or 'on the other hand' about it. In our text example, the ground floor is being contrasted with the roof—'you might expect the roof to leak, but not the lower part of the house'. In complex structures this tone is often associated with the meaning 'if'.

Tone 5 is the converse of tone 4: rise followed by fall. The origin is 'it may not seem clearcut, but it is'. This tone, which is very commonly used by children, has a sense of 'of course', 'for sure', often with the nuance of 'you ought to have known that'. It is particularly associated with exclamations.

So the general meaning of the choice of tone is: this is the 'key' of this particular move in the discourse. We can set it up as a system of alternatives, as in Figure 4.3. This presents a synoptic view: the 'meaning potential' that is carried by the resources of tone in English. (For a more detailed account, see my *Intonation and Grammar in British English.*) In the next section, we will treat tone and tonicity together from a dynamic point of view.

Figure 4.3 A general model of the meaning of the English tones

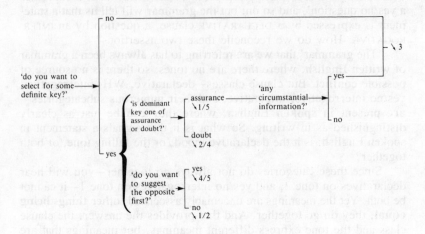

The dynamics of intonation

As we observed earlier, connected English speech consists of an unbroken succession of melodic units (tone groups); each one is a sequence of one or more rhythmic units (feet), is characterised by a particular melodic contour (tone), and has one point of prominence, sometimes two, where maximum melodic movement takes place (tonic nucleus). This prosodic patterning is meaningful: the location of the tonic realises the information structure, and the choice of tone realises the key.

There are no pauses between tone groups, nor are their boundaries definitively marked; a tone group is considered to continue up to the foot that marks the onset of the next one. This may be either a tonic foot (tone 1, 2, 3, 4, or 5) or a pretonic foot.

We shall not describe the pretonic segment in detail. With each tone is associated a small range of pretonic contours which have the function of (1) marking the beginning of the information unit and (2) adding further specification of the key. There is usually a rather clear distinction between starting a new tone group and going on with the old one: if there are further feet after the tonic foot but in the same tone group, they form a 'tail'—they simply maintain the pitch movement of the tonic, but less steeply, like the words *likely to leak* in Figure 4.2. If on the other hand the speaker is beginning the pretonic segment of a new tone group, he is likely to jump in pitch either up or down. If we altered that example to read

> Why are there floods in houses? I should have thought the roof would keep the rain away

we might expect a new pretonic to begin at *keep*, and to be marked by an upjump as in Figure 4.4.

In discourse, each step defines a context from which the next one begins. Imagine a beginning. In real life there are few real beginnings, since most conversations are in some sense continuings of conversations that have taken place before; but we can accept the notion of the starting point of a conversation. Its context is the context of situation: the features of field, tenor, and mode which determine the kinds of meanings that will be exchanged.

Figure 4.4 Another intonation contour

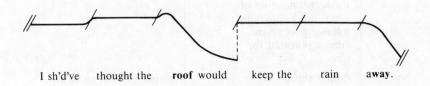

I sh'd've   thought the   **roof** would   keep the   rain   **away.**

From the moment that there is an environment—some culturally recognised activity is going on, such as an outing; some interpersonal roles and statuses are defined, for example, pensioners interacting with each other and with a tour guide; and some rhetorical mode is adopted, for example, spoken, free conversation—a member of the culture can make predictions about the language that will follow, with a better-than-chance probability of being right. There are expectations from the start: set phrases lining up to be produced, and parts of the linguistic system primed ready for access.

Once conversation starts, a new element is added: each new step defines the environment afresh. The meaning of whatever is said is 'with respect' to what has gone before. The process is a stochastic one: the probabilities are reset at each boundary, and the linguistic resources regrouped to face the new situation. This is not something that happens merely between one turn and another (one speaker and the next). It is perhaps easiest to think of in the context of dialogue, because there we readily accept that the interactant who is listening has to wait to hear what the one who is speaking says; but the one who is speaking also has to wait to hear what he himself says—it is not all mapped out before he starts. As in many of the phenomena we study, the macro picture is predictable, but the micro behaviour is highly variable.

intonation and the flow of discourse; how each move changes the context for what is to follow

Every language is organised so as to cope with this kind of demand, and this is the particular significance of the prosodic systems we are discussing. (The other resource that is specially called on to carry the dynamics of spoken language is that of taxis; this is described in Chapter 6.) The combination of tone, tonicity, and rhythm enables the speaker (or speakers—the principle holds **whether discourse is shared or not**, and it does not much matter when and how often there is a change of turn) to go on creating meaning without becoming irrelevant. (This is not to suggest, of course, that speakers always achieve this estimable goal; the point is that the resources are there.) He can indicate which are the content-bearing elements, vary the density with which new information is introduced, show how it relates to what has gone before, give it a particular 'key signature' to indicate its relevance at this particular point—and direct the listener exactly to what he wants him to attend to.

Let us tabulate these for ease of reference (see Table 4.3).

59

Table 4.3 Functions of rhythm and intonation in English

	function in discourse	other systematic functions
rhythm	highlights content words (lexical items); creates potential for tonicity and tone	distinguishes structures e.g. defining and non-defining relatives
tonicity	highlights element under focus (culmination of new); marks anything following as given; creates potential for tone	
tone	(tonic) signals key; also certain logical relations [see below]	combines with mood to signal semantic categories of rhetorical function
	(pretonic) marks onset of new tone group; signals subcategories of key	

We end this chapter with a transcription of part of a conversation (recorded and transcribed by Afaf Elmenoufy).

A: //4 ˰ the / only real / **accident** that //4 I've ever / **had** was //1 ˰ in fog and / **ice** and //1 ˰ there was . . . a //13 big / **truck** / parked on the / side of the / **road** a//1 bout . . . / three / **feet** a//1 **way** from the / side of the / road and it was //1 very / **thick** / fog //4 ˰ and a / **mini** had //1 gone into / this / **truck** //4 ˰ well the / **mini** had just //1 touched the / **offside** of the / truck with its //1 nearside / **wing** and so it //4 meant when / **I** came a/long //4 **my** side of the / road was com//1 pletely / **blocked** and //4 ˰ un/**fortunately** I //1 went into a / four wheel / **skid** be//4 fore coming / up to this / **mini** and //4 ˰ at / **that** time I //1 didn't / know how to / **deal** with a / four wheel / skid and //4 ˰ so / I went / into / the / **mini** //

B: //1 ˰ you / hit it / sideways / **on** //

A: //3 ˰ a/bout / twelve / cars / went into / **me** and //3 then / ˰ a / friend of / **ours** //3 came a/**long** and //1 he de/cided to / try and / overtake the / **lot** and so he //1 went / into / each / **one** sort of //1 banging them / **sideways** as it / were and //1 oh / this was in / **daylight** //

B: //1 ˰ be/cause of the / **fog** //

A: //4 needless to / **say** I //4 treat / **fog** with //13 **great** re/spect / **now** //

B: //1 yes I //1 **know** they //53 keep / **happening** these / multiple col/lisions in / **fog** //2 were you all / **right** though as a re/sult of / **this** //

A: //1 oh / **yes** //1 oh / **yes** there //4 ˰ there was / no-one / **injured** //

60

Chapter 5

Written language: lexical density

The complexity of written language

The following sentence is taken from a written report (*Annual Report of the National Trust of Australia 1982–83*, p.14):

> The Trust has offered advice to local government authorities on cemetery conservation.

It consists of twelve words. Of these, eight are lexical items (content words) and four are grammatical items (function words). Grammatical items are those that function in closed systems in the language: in English, determiners, pronouns, most prepositions, conjunctions, some classes of adverb, and finite verbs. (Determiners include the articles.) In this example, the grammatical words are *the*, *has*, *to*, and *on*.

grammatical ('function') words and lexical ('content') words

In other words, there are twice as many lexical words as there are grammatical words. Compare this with the first part of the spoken text at the end of the last chapter:

> The only real accident that I've ever had was in fog and ice.

Counting I've as one word, this has 13 words; of these, *the*, *only*, *that*, *I've*, *ever*, *had*, *was*, *in*, and *and* are grammatical items; the lexical items are *real*, *accident*, *fog*, and *ice*. Here the proportions are reversed: twice as many grammatical as lexical.

This is a characteristic difference between spoken and written language. Written language displays a much higher ratio of lexical items to total running words.

This is not just a consequence of the subject-matter. Here are a number of written sentences with a 'translation' into a form that would be more likely to occur in speech; it is still not specially 'colloquial'. Figures show the numbers of lexical (L) and grammatical (G) words.

Investment in a rail facility implies a long-term commitment. (L:7; G:3)	If you invest in a rail facility, this implies that you are going to be committed for a long term. (L:7; G:13)

61

The growth of attachment between infant and mother signals the first step in the development of a child's capacity to discriminate amongst people. (L:12; G:11)	When an infant and its mother start to grow attached to each other, this is a sign that the child is beginning to discriminate amongst people. (L:10; G:16)
Business community lunchers relax in this dappled midcity sanctuary while saving something for the resident seagulls. (L:10; G:6)	Members of the business community relax while they lunch in this dappled sanctuary in the middle of the city, and save something for the seagulls who live there. (L:12; G:16)
She said such an exercise had the potential for intrusions by the government into the legitimate privacy of non-government schools. (L:10; G:10)	She said if that was done it would make it possible for the government to intrude into non-governmental schools, which had a right to their own privacy. (L:10; G:17)
Some migrants acted upon encouraging advice from relatives and friends who had preceded them to the colonies. (L:8; G:9)	Some people migrated because they were encouraged by the advice they got from their relatives and friends who had gone to the colonies before them. (L: 9; G:16)
Slavish imitation of models is nowhere implied. (L:4; G:3)	It is not implied anywhere that there are models which should be slavishly imitated. (L:4; G:10)
A grey-faced Dr Coffin unlocked the door. (L:6; G:2)	Dr Coffin unlocked the door, and as he did so his face was grey. (L:5; G:9)

We can explain the significance of this distinction as follows. The difference between written and spoken language is one of DENSITY: the density with which the information is presented. Relative to each other, written language is dense, spoken language is sparse.

A number of factors contribute to this density; it is a fairly complex phenomenon, as we would discover if we tried to quantify it in an exact way. But it is mainly the product of a small number of variables, and these we can observe without a complicated battery of measurements.

One caution should be given. By expressing the distinction in this way, we have already 'loaded' it semantically. To say that written language is 'more dense' is to suggest that, if we start from spoken language, then written language will be shown to be more complex.

the kind of complexity that is typical of written language: 'lexical density'.

We could have looked at the same phenomenon from the other end. We could have said that the difference between spoken language and written language is one of intricacy, the intricacy with which the information is organised. Spoken language is more intricate than written.

In the next chapter, we shall look into the phenomenon of intricacy—which is in fact a related phenomenon, but seen from the opposite perspective. From that point of view, it will appear that spoken language is more complex than written. The conclusion will be that each is complex in its own way. Written language displays one kind of complexity, spoken language another. Our aim will be to make clear what these are.

62

After considering both kinds of complexity, we shall try to account for them under a single generalisation. This will relate to the concept of lexico-grammar: the level of 'wording' in language. One way of expressing the matter—rather oversimplified, but it provides a pointer in the right direction—is that the complexity of written language is lexical, while that of spoken language is grammatical.

What we are examining now, therefore, with the notion of 'density', is a kind of complexity that arises in the deployment of words.

Lexical density

The distinction we have to recognise at this point is one we have referred to already: that between lexical items and grammatical items. Lexical items are often called 'content words'. Technically, they are ITEMS (i.e. constituents of variable length) rather than words in the usual sense, because they may consist of more than one word: for example, *stand up*, *take over*, *call off*, and other phrasal verbs all function as single lexical items. They are LEXICAL because they function in lexical sets not grammatical systems: that is to say, they enter into open not closed contrasts.

A grammatical item enters into a closed system. For example, the personal pronoun *him* contrasts on one dimension with *he*, *his*; on another dimension with *me*, *you*, *her*, *it*, *us*, *them*, *one*; but that is all. There are no more items in these classes and we cannot add any. With a lexical item, however, we cannot close off its class membership; it enters into an open set, which is indefinitely extendable. So the word *door* is in contrast with *gate* and *screen*; also with *window*, *wall*, *floor* and *ceiling*; with *knob*, *handle*, *panel*, and *sill*; with *room*, *house*, *hall*; with *entrance*, *opening*, *portal*—there is no way of closing off the sets of items that it is related to, and new items can always come into the picture.

the concept of a 'lexical item'

As you would expect, there is a continuum from lexis into grammar: while many items in a language are clearly of one kind or the other, there are always likely to be intermediate cases. In English, prepositions and certain classes of adverb (for example, MODAL adverbs like *always*, *perhaps*) are on this borderline. For purposes of comparing spoken and written English it does not matter exactly where we draw the line provided we do it consistently.

Like many other features of language, the distinction is quite clear in our unconscious understanding (which is never troubled by border-line cases, unlike our conscious mind). Children are clearly well aware of it—one of the developmental strategies used by many children for constructing sentences in the mother tongue is to leave out all gram-matical items; and some children re-use this strategy when first learning to write (see Mackay et al. 1978).

We have already pointed out that the distinction is embodied in our spelling system, since grammatical items may have only one or two letters in them, whereas lexical items require a minimum of three (showing incidentally that prepositions, at least the common ones, belong in the 'grammatical' class, because of words like *at*, *in*, *to*, *on*, which otherwise would have to be spelt *att*, *inn*, *too*, *onn*). And there are some 'special languages' around the world that are based entirely on this distinction, since they require all lexical items to be altered while all grammatical ones remain unchanged—for example the mother-in-law language in Dyirbal, North Queensland (see Dixon 1980). So it is not surprising that the distinction is fundamental to the difference between speech and writing.

In principle a grammatical item has no place in a dictionary. But our tradition of dictionary-making is to include all words, grammatical as well as lexical; so the dictionary solemnly enters *the* and *it*, even though it has nothing to say about them—nothing, that is, that falls within the scope of lexicology. A more consistent practice is that of *Roget's Thesaurus*, which does leave out most of the grammatical words; those that are included are there because Roget treats them lexically, for example lining up *me* with *personality*, *ego*, *spirit* (and not with *you* and *us*).

lexical density (1): the number of lexical items as a proportion of the number of running words

As a first approximation to a measure of lexical density, therefore, we can draw the distinction between lexical and grammatical items, simplifying it by treating each **word** (in the sense of what is treated as a word in the writing system, being written with a space on either side) as the relevant item, and counting the ratio of lexical to grammatical words. We then express this as a proportion of the total number of running words. If there are 12 lexical and 8 grammatical items, this gives the proportion of lexical items to the total as 12 out of 20, which we show as a lexical density of 60 per cent, or 0.6. In general, the more 'written' the language being used, the higher will be the proportion of lexical words to the total number of running words in the text.

Frequency

The next thing to take account of is probability.

Another aspect of the distinction between lexical and grammatical words is that grammatical items tend to be considerably more frequent in occurrence. A list of the most frequently occurring words in the English language will always be headed by grammatical items like *the* and *and* and *it*. Lexical items are repeated much less often.

This in itself is entirely predictable, and of no great significance to the present point. What is significant is the relative frequency of one lexical item to another.

We have been assuming a simple measure in which all lexical items count the same. But the actual effect that we are responding to is one in which the relative frequency of the item plays a significant part. The relative frequency of grammatical items can be ignored, since all of them fall into the relatively frequent bracket. But the relative frequency of lexical items is an important factor in the situation.

The vocabulary of every language includes a number of highly frequent words, often general terms for large classes of phenomena. Examples from English are *thing*, *people*, *way*, *do*, *make*, *get*, *have*, *go*, *good*, *many*. These are lexical items, but on the borderline of grammar; they often perform functions that are really grammatical—for example *thing* as a general noun (almost a pronoun) as in *that's a thing I could well do without*; *make* as a general verb, as in *you make me tired, it makes no difference*. They therefore contribute very little to the lexical density.

By contrast, a lexical item of rather low frequency in the language contributes a great deal. Clearly there is a difference between the following examples in the feeling of density that they give: compare

the mechanism of sex determination varies in different organisms

with

the way the sex is decided differs with different creatures

or

different creatures have their sex decided in different ways.

the relative expectedness of a word when it occurs, and the effect of this on lexical density

The proportion of lexical items is about the same in all three; but the last two 'feel' less dense because they include very frequent items such as *have* and *way*.

Another factor that operates here is that the last two examples incorporate a repetition, the item *differ/different*. Repetition also reduces the effect of density—since even if a word is intrinsically rare, its occurrence sets up the expectation that it will occur again. Note that normally all the members of a morphological paradigm are the same lexical item: for example, *differ, differed, different, difference, differing, differently* are all instances of the one lexical item (but not *differential* in *differential equation*). This is another difference between 'lexical item' and 'word'.

For a systematic, formal investigation of lexical density in texts we should have to adopt some weighting whereby lexical items of lower frequency 'scored' more highly than common ones. Word-frequency lists have been available for some time, and there are now large bodies of written and spoken text in machine-readable form in various places from which such information can readily be obtained.

But for immediate practical purposes, either all lexical items can be treated alike—this will still show up the difference between spoken and written texts—or a list can be drawn up of high-frequency lexical items to be given half of the value of the others. This is equivalent to recognising three categories rather than two: grammatical items, high-frequency lexical items, and low-frequency lexical items.

A more revealing measure of lexical density

So far we have assumed that the feature of lexical density was just something to do with words. The measurements we have suggested have been concerned with the pattern of distribution of words of different kinds in spoken and written texts. We started with a classification of all words into two categories—grammatical and lexical—and envisaged the possibility of refining this by taking into account the frequency of a word in the language (i.e. its unconditioned probability of occurrence at any point)—either crudely, but enough to allow for the much greater effect of low-frequency lexical items, or more delicately by building in a differential system of weightings for all.

However far we took such refinements, we should still be measuring words against words. But this is rather one-sided, because it suggests that spoken language is simply to be characterised by a negative feature, the relative absence of (or low level of) density of information. Is there any way of reinterpreting this notion so that it tells us something positive about spoken language as well?

Let us examine the notion of density further. It has to do, as already suggested, with how closely packed the information is. This is why the probability of the item is important: a word of low probability carries more information. But words are not packed inside other words; they are packaged in larger grammatical units—sentences, and their component parts. It is this packaging into larger grammatical structures that really determines the informational density of a passage of text.

Which is the most relevant of these larger structures? There is one that clearly stands out as the unit where meanings are organised and wrapped up together, and that is the CLAUSE. The clause is the grammatical unit in which semantic constructs of different kinds are brought together and integrated into a whole.

clause, sentence, and 'clause complex'

This always appears a difficult notion at first, because of the inconsistency with which the terms 'clause' and 'sentence' are used in traditional grammars. But in fact it is not excessively complicated. If we take as our starting point the observation that a so-called 'simple sentence' is a sentence **consisting of one clause**, then much of the difficulty disappears. What is traditionally known as a 'compound sentence' will still consist of two or more clauses; and each of them potentially carries the same load of information as the single clause of a 'simple sentence'.

Eventually we shall discard the term 'sentence' from the grammar altogether; it can then be used unambiguously to refer to a unit of the **writing system**—that which extends from a capital letter following a full stop up to the next full stop. In place of 'sentence' in the grammar we shall use CLAUSE COMPLEX, because that will allow us to refer both to written and to spoken language in a way that makes the two comparable. We cannot identify a 'sentence' in the spoken language; or rather, we can identify a sentence in spoken language only by defining it as a clause complex. And since the notion of a 'complex' can be formally defined, and yields not only clause complexes but also phrase complexes, group complexes, and word complexes, it seems simpler to adopt this term throughout.

The clause complex is, in fact, what the sentence (in writing) comes from. The unit that was intuitively recognised by our ancestors when they first introduced the 'stop' as a punctuation mark was the clause complex; that is, a sequence of clauses all structurally linked.

For our notation, we will use three vertical strokes to mark a sentence boundary (still using the term 'sentence' pro tem; but gradually phasing it out), and two vertical strokes to mark a clause boundary. For example:

||| The basic 'stuff' of living organisms is protoplasm. ||| There is no set composition of this || and it varies between one individual and the next. |||

The clause is the gateway from the semantics to the grammar. It provides a more powerful and more relevant organising concept for

66

measuring lexical density, and, more generally, for enabling us to capture the special properties of both spoken and written language. Instead of counting the number of lexical items as a ratio of the total number of running words, we will count the number of lexical items as a ratio of the total number of clauses. LEXICAL DENSITY will be measured as the number of lexical items per clause.

lexical density (2): the number of lexical items as a ratio of the number of clauses

Keeping to the simplest classification (each word is either a lexical item or a grammatical item), the three clauses in the above text contain, respectively, five (*basic*, *stuff*, *living*, *organisms*, *protoplasm*), two (*set*, *composition*), and two (*varies*, *individual*) lexical items; a total of nine, giving an average of three per clause. We will therefore say that this text has a mean lexical density of 3.0.

The clause

What we are measuring, then, for any text, spoken or written, is the average amount of lexical information per clause. No account need be taken, for purposes of this particular measurement, of the number and organisation of clauses in the sentence (clause complex). But it will be necessary to identify explicitly what is a clause.

It is not always easy, however, to recognise what a clause is. Again, for comparative purposes, the main requirement is consistency; but since this category is perhaps the most fundamental category in the whole of lingusitics, as well as being critical to the **unity** of spoken and written language, it is important to devote a section to the discussion of it.

Precisely because it is so fundamental a category, the clause is also impossible to define; nor is there just one right way of describing it. Being so complex and many-sided, it lends itself to different theoretical interpretations; there are very many different kinds of generalisation that a linguist may be interested in, for different purposes, and the clause is likely to come out looking somewhat different in each case. But all interpretations will also have something in common.

The brief outline given below represents an interpretation that I have found useful in the general context of educational linguistics. It is a theoretical interpretation with a strongly pragmatic motive behind it, derived from two complementary aspects of experience—that theories are developed for the purpose of being applied, but that unless you develop a theory you will not have anything to apply. The principal purposes for which this interpretation has been used are text analysis, from natural conversation to literature; the study of functional variation (register) in language; language teaching, including mother tongue and foreign language; child language development; and artificial intelligence research.

According to this interpretation, the clause is a functional unit with a triple construction of meaning: it functions simultaneously (1) as the representation of the phenomena of experience, as these are interpreted by the members of the culture; (2) as the expression of speech function, through the categories of mood described in Chapter 4; and (3) as the bearer of the message, which is organised in the form of theme plus exposition.

defining the clause by reference to its threefold function

To each of these functions corresponds a structural configuration,

(1) in terms of a process (action, event, behaviour, mental process, verbal process, existence, or relation) together with participants in the process and circumstances attendant on it ('Medium', Agent, Beneficiary, Time, Cause, etc.); (2) in terms of an element embodying an arguable proposition (Subject plus Finite) and residual elements (Predicator, Complement, and Adjunct); (3) in terms of a thematic element, given prominence as what the message is about, and a residual element (summarised as the 'Rheme'). In addition, (4) the clause provides a reference point for the information structure in spoken discourse, closely related to (3)—there is systematic interplay between the Theme − Rheme organisation of the clause and the Given − New organisation of the information unit (realised as a tone group) (for details see Halliday 1985).

An example of the analysis of a clause in these terms is given in Figure 5.1.

Figure 5.1 Analysis of a clause

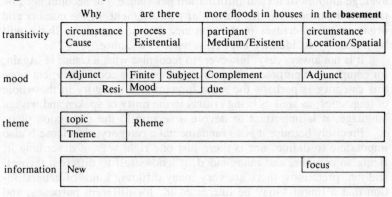

The 'systems' (sets of options that embody the choices in meaning) that are expressed through the various functional configurations (1), (2), and (3) above are, respectively, those of TRANSITIVITY, MOOD, and THEME. Let us tabulate the principal categories that come under the first two of these headings (see Table 5.1). (We shall return to the concept of theme at a later point.)

A clause, then, can be defined as the locus of choices in transitivity, mood, and theme. This does not imply that all choices under these headings are open to all clauses; they are not. But every clause embodies **some** pattern of selection in these three functional components of the grammar.

In the developmental perspective, picking up what was being discussed in the first chapter, the systems of mood and transitivity are the **evolved** reflexes of the child's twofold functional demands on language. Mood has evolved out of the requirement that language should serve as a means of action, a way of exchanging goods-and-services and information. Transitivity has evolved out of the requirement that language should serve as a means of reflection, a way of learning and knowing about the world. And the clause has evolved out of the need to combine the two functions in a single semiotic act.

the clause as the locus of transitivity, mood, and theme

68

Table 5.1 Principal categories of transitivity and mood in English

System	Options	Elements of structure	Class by which typically realised
transitivity	material (action, event) behavioural mental (perception, affection, cognition) verbal relational (attributive, identifying) existential	process	verbal group
		participants (Medium, Agent, Beneficiary, Range, Attribute)	nominal group
		circumstances (Extent, Location, Cause, Manner, Accompaniment, Matter, Role)	adverbial group or prepositional phrase
mood	declarative yes/no interrogative WH-interrogative imperative	Subject; Complement	nominal group
		Finite Predicator	verbal group
		Adjunct	adverbial group or prepositional phrase

It can be seen that the amount of lexical information that may be incorporated into a clause is extremely varied. There may be none at all, in a clause such as *Don't!* or *It is*. There may be a very great deal, as in

> The most advantageous shell colours are yellow in green areas, pink on leaf litter, and reds and browns in beach woods with red litter and numerous exposures of blackish soil.
>
> (C. Jarman, *Evolution of Life*,
> Sun Books, Melbourne, 1970, p.70)

which has nineteen lexical items in it. It is precisely the great flexibility of the clause in this respect that has made possible the evolution of written forms of discourse.

The clause as an elastic body

If the clause can accommodate such large quantities of lexical information, it must have considerable elasticity. Let us see where its flexible points are.

Consider the following clause (from Bertrand Russell's *ABC of Relativity*, George Allen & Unwin, London, 1969, p.118):

> In the Newtonian system, bodies under the action of no forces move in straight lines with uniform velocity.

69

We need to introduce one more notational convention: a single vertical line separating elements of clause structure:

|| in the Newtonian system | bodies under the action of no forces | move | in straight lines | with uniform velocity ||

1. Out of the ten lexical items, all except *bodies* and *move* occur in prepositional phrases. The prepositional phrases may function (1) as circumstantial elements in the clause, or (2) as postmodifying elements in the nominal group.

   Here the circumstantial phrases are *in the Newtonian system* (location), *in straight lines* (manner), *with uniform velocity* (manner).

   The postmodifying phrases are *under the action of no forces* and *of no forces*. How does this work? (1) *of no forces* is a postmodifier in the nominal group *the action of no forces*, of which the head noun is *action*. (2) *under the action of no forces* is postmodifier in the nominal group *bodies under the action of no forces*, of which *bodies* is the head noun. We can represent this diagrammatically as in Figure 5.2.

Figure 5.2 Typical structure of postmodifying elements in the nominal group

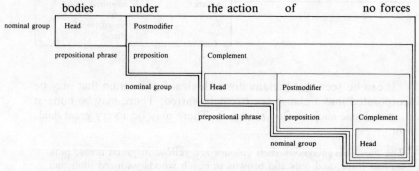

Figure 5.2 shows how the prepositional phrase can occur many times in a single clause: (1) by having a circumstantial function in the clause itself, (2) by having a postmodifying function inside a nominal group functioning in the clause.

nominal groups and prepositional phrases

2. Now let us turn to the nominal group. Likewise, a nominal group may function (1) as a participant in the clause, and (2) as a participant in a prepositional phrase. In this example we have
   (a) bodies under the action of no forces   (in clause)
   (b) the Newtonian system   (in prepositional phrase)
       the action of no forces   "
       no forces   "
       straight lines   "
       uniform velocity   "
   — in other words, six nominal groups, five of them functioning inside prepositional phrases.

   There is therefore a recursive principle at work in the clause, such that nominal groups can function inside prepositional phrases and prepositional phrases can function inside nominal groups. Such elements are said to be 'down-ranked' or 'embedded'. This structure can accommodate a great deal of lexical material.

70

3. Later in the same paragraph we find
   ‖ our apparent imaginative understanding of these processes
   | is | quite fallacious ‖‖

Here there is a nominal group *our apparent imaginative understanding of these processes*, which also contains a prepositional phrase as postmodifier *of these processes*, which in turn contains a nominal group, *these processes*, on the same principle as those above.

   But this nominal group also has lexical items **before** the head, in premodifying function: *apparent*, *imaginative*. These premodifying sequences can be considerably longer:
   the current nineteenth-century analytical procedures
   natural whole wheat biscuits
   timber promotion council small diameter timber pile research project

4. And some way below that, there is a clause containing the nominal group
   | a physicist who has assumed the formula for interval which is used in the special theory of relativity |

Here again it is the postmodifying element that contains the lexical information: the whole wording is one nominal group with head *physicist*. The postmodifier is, as usual, embedded; but here it is by a down-ranked **clause**, functioning as a defining relative clause beginning at *who*. This relative clause, in turn, contains a nominal group *the formula for interval which is used in the special theory of relativity*; this has head *formula* and two postmodifying elements, both embedded—the prepositional phrase *for interval* and the defining relative clause *which is used in the special theory of relativity* (which in turn contains a prepositional phrase with a nominal group *the special theory of relativity* as complement; and this in its turn has both a pre- and a post-modifier in it).

   Let us now represent all of these using an additional symbol to show embedding: | | for a down-ranked group or phrase, ‖ ‖ for a down-ranked clause. The examples in (1)–(4) will appear as follows:
   ‖ in [N the Newtonian system]N bodies [under [N the action [of [N no forces | move | in [N straight lines]] with [N uniform velocity]]‖
   ‖N our apparent imaginative understanding [of [N these processes]]| is |N quite fallacious ‖
   ‖N he | supposes |N a physicist [[N who | has assumed |N the formula [for [N interval]] which | is used | in [N the special theory [of [N relativity]]]]]‖‖

   In this instance I have added a small N at the beginning of each constituent that is a nominal group. This will show which of the lexical items occur in nominal groups and which occur outside them. In these three examples the picture is as follows:

- in nominal groups: Newtonian, system, bodies, action, forces, straight, lines, uniform, velocity; apparent, imaginative, understanding, processes, fallacious; physicist, formula, interval, special, theory, relativity.
- in verbal groups: move; is; supposes, assumed, used.

71

almost all lexicalised 'content' carried in nominal groups

In other words, the overwhelming proportion of 'content', in the sense of lexicalised meaning, is carried in the nominal groups—by nouns and their premodifying nouns and adjectives. In these three clauses, there are five verbs, all high-frequency items carrying little lexical information; and two of those (*assume, use*) are in clauses that are themselves embedded in nominal groups. All the meat of the message is in the nominals.

Nouns and nominality

It is commonly said of modern English, usually in rather disparaging terms, that it is a 'highly nominalised' language—or, at least, that if the language is not inherently nominalised, people use it that way.

I have chosen examples from Bertrand Russell because I do not think he is someone who would normally be criticised for having an over-nominalised style. Yet in these extracts—which are not untypical—it is clear that the lexical meaning is largely carried in the nouns. Is there any reason for this?

Essentially there are two reasons, both to be found within the grammar of English. One is the structure of the nominal group; the other is the structure of the clause.

The structure of the nominal group

The nominal group consists of a Head that may be preceded and/or followed by modifying elements—premodifiers and postmodifiers. Their functions can be illustrated as follows (see Figure 5.3).

Figure 5.3 Structure of a nominal group

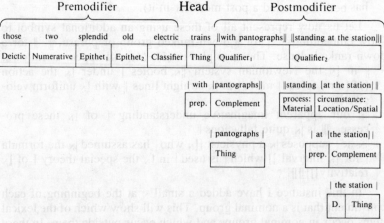

the internal structure of the nominal group, contrasted with that of the verbal group

In addition to the Head noun, which represents the 'Thing'—the class of phenomena being referred to—there are other functions, those of Classifier and Epithet, which also contain lexical information: the subclass (*electric trains* as opposed to *steam* or *diesel*) and qualities of various kinds (for example, *old*), including those expressing the speaker's attitude (for example, *splendid*). All these are present without

72

embedding; if in addition we add down-ranked prepositional phrases and clauses, as Qualifiers, then each of these opens up the possibility of further nominal groups, which in turn may contain Epithets or Classifiers; and so forth.

Verbal groups, on the other hand, contain only one lexical element: the verb itself. Other lexical material may be expressed in adverbial groups; but these are very limited in scope. About the only nominal group in these clauses that could have been replaced by an adverbial group is (*with*) *uniform velocity*, where we might have had *steadily fast*; but it is not very easy—all the expressions usually used in this general sense encode 'fast' as a noun and 'steadily' as an adjective: (*with*) *uniform velocity*, (*at*) *constant speed*, (*at*) *a steady pace*, and so on.

Thus there are a lot of things that can only be said in nominal constructions; especially in registers that have to do with the world of science and technology, where things, and the ideas behind them, are multiplying and proliferating all the time. That is to say; they can only be said this way **in the grammar of modern English**. The question whether the grammar had to evolve this way in order to say them is a fundamental issue that, regretfully, would require a whole further treatise to itself. And even then we would not find the answer.

The structure of the clause

As far as the structure of the clause is concerned, there is another source of pressure towards nominalisation. This has to do with the category of theme, which was referred to briefly above.

In addition to its organisation as representation of a process (transitivity) and as bearer of a speech function (mood), every clause is also structured as a message. It consists of two parts: a Theme, which is the point of departure—what the message is about; and another element that constitutes the body of the message, known as the Rheme.

In some languages there are special particles for indicating what is the Theme. In English, the message structure is expressed by word order: the Theme comes first.

The Theme itself can be a fairly complex structure, but what concerns us here is the topical element within it—the portion that functions in transitivity. In the examples above, the topical component of the Theme is (1) *in the Newtonian system*, (2) *our apparent imaginative understanding of these processes*, and (3) *he*.

the thematic structure of the clause

The Theme is an important part of the message, since it is here that the speaker announces his intentions: the peg on which the message is to hang. In spoken language it is often a pronoun, most typically *I* or *you*. But in writing, with its more strongly 'third person' orientation, it is usually some other phenomenon; and again this is typically a nominal element.

It cannot, except in special circumstances, be a verbal group; so this is another reason why lexical material tends to be packaged in nouns. It can be a prepositional phrase, as in (1) above; but here, as we have already seen, the content is in the nominal group that is embedded inside it. It can be an adverbial group; but these, as has been observed, have a fairly limited semantic scope.

Furthermore, there is a special structure in English that has evolved as a means of packaging the message in the desired thematic form. These are what in formal grammars are called 'cleft' and 'pseudo-cleft' constructions. Consider the clause (made up for purposes of the discussion) *the force of gravity attracts the planets to the sun*. Let us suppose, now, that we want to vary this message in different ways. There are many possibilities; we will illustrate two.

1. Suppose we want the *force of gravity* to be the focus of information, the New element in the information structure. If we were **saying** this, we could say it as

//1 ˰ the / force of / **gravity** at/tracts the / planets to the / sun //

In writing we cannot do this; instead we assume an unmarked information structure, with the New at the end, and write

The planets are attracted to the sun by the force of gravity.

This will now be 'read' with the focus on *gravity*. However, we have now disturbed the thematic structure; instead of *the force of gravity* being Theme, the Theme is now *the planets*. If the writer wants to have *the force of gravity* both as Theme and as New ('this is what I'm talking about—and it's also what I want you particularly to attend to'), he introduces a special structural device for PREDICATING the Theme:

It is the force of gravity that attracts the planets to the sun.

This puts the tonic back on *gravity*.

2. Suppose on the other hand that the writer (or speaker, in this case; here both will need a resource for the purpose) wants to have, not just *the planets* as Theme but the whole of *the planets are attracted to the sun*: 'I want to tell you about planet-to-sun attraction'. The only way of achieving this is to package all of these up together:

What attracts the planets to the sun is the force of gravity.

This has the effect of making the whole of *what attracts the planets to the sun* into the Theme, and then IDENTIFYING this Theme, by means of the verb *be*, with *the force of gravity* as Rheme.

Let us set these out with the structural notation:

(a) ‖ it ǀ is ǀ the force of gravity ǀ ⟦ that attracts the planets to the sun ⟧ ‖
(b) ‖ ⟦ what attracts the planets to the sun ⟧ ǀ is ǀ the force of gravity ‖

In (b), *what attracts the planets to the sun* is both Theme and Subject. In (a), the Subject is again *it . . . that attracts the planets to the sun*; but the Theme is *the force of gravity*. This is what is known as a 'marked' Theme: one that has special prominence precisely because it is **not** the Subject.

In both these cases, the writer has depended on NOMINALISATION to get the meaning he wants. In other words, even things that are not expressed as nouns have to **behave like** nouns in order to gain their appropriate status in the thematic and information structure. This is the second of the kinds of pressure that tend towards nominalised forms

Dressing up as a noun is the only way to gain access to all the possibilities in thematic and informational structure.

74

of expression in English. In order to exploit the full potential of the language for mapping any transitivity structure—any configuration of process, participants, and circumstances—on to any desired message structure (Theme and Rheme, Given and New, in all their possible combinations), one has to be prepared to express oneself in a nominalised form.

So the structure of the modern world and the structure of the language combine together to make the written language what it is: a language with a high lexical density, measured in the number (and informational load) of lexical items per clause, and a strong tendency to encode this lexical content in a nominal form: in head nouns, other items (nouns and adjectives) in the nominal group, and nominalised clauses. It is these nominal structures that give the clause its enormous elasticity.

This is not to say they are never overused: it is always possible to overdo a good thing. But it is important, if one is critical of such tendencies, to understand how the patterns in question are functional in the language.

Chapter 6

Spoken language: grammatical intricacy

Speech no less structured than writing

It is time to return to the spoken language, and to ask: what does the spoken language do instead? Is it merely characterised by the absence of certain features that are found in writing, or has it got particular characteristics of its own?

There is a tradition of regarding spoken language as formless and featureless. Thus for example:

> Spontaneous speech is unlike written text. It contains many mistakes, sentences are usually brief and indeed the whole fabric of verbal expression is riddled with hesitations and silences. To take a very simple example: in a seminar which I recorded, an articulate (and well-known) linguist was attempting to say the following:
>
> > No, I'm coming back to the judgements question. Indeterminacy appears to be rife. I don't think it is, if one sorts out which are counterexamples to judgement.
>
> But what he actually said was:
>
> > No *I'm saying* I'm coming back to the judgements question (267) *you know there appear to* (200) *ah* indeterminacy (1467) appears to be rife. I don't think it is (200) *if one* (267) if one sorts out which are counterexamples (267) to judgement, I mean observing.
>
> Here, the brief silences (unfilled pauses) have been measured in milliseconds and marked (these are the numbers in brackets) and all other types of hesitation—false starts, repetitions, filled pauses and parenthetic remarks put in italics. It is these hesitations (both filled and unfilled) which dominate spontaneous speech and give it its distinctive structure and feeling.
>
> (Geoffrey Beattie: *Talk: An Analysis of Speech and Non-verbal Behaviour in Conversation*, Open University Press, 1983, p.33)

All this amounts to is that in speech you cannot destroy the earlier drafts. If we had access to Mr Beattie's original manuscript or type-script, and published that with all the crossingsout, misspellings, redraftings, and periods of silent thought measured in thirtieths of a second, we could say 'But what he actually wrote was . . .'

the myth of the formlessness of spoken language

Here is another example:

'Yer saw the *Star Trek* film, eh? What ya think of it then?'
'Oh, dunno. S'alright I s'pose [*shrugs expressively*] . . . good effects
. . . yeah . . . beaut effects. And they've got these things . . . these
spaceships . . . sort of sailing along . . . and the music . . . wow, that
was something. But it wasn't all that . . . [*Waves hand disparagingly*]
you know . . .'
'Boring?'
'Yeah . . . no . . . what I mean is . . . well in *Star Wars* they were
really up against something, weren't they . . . it got you in, didn't it?
don't you reckon? Yeah, but in this film . . . well, there's no one there
when they get there. Too much . . . no, too little, happens . . . I dunno
. . . give me *Star Wars*'.

Did you notice how formless, tentative and spur-of-the-moment
the sample of speech . . . was? Yet, although it looks shabby in
printed form, the original conversation would have seemed quite
sensible to the participants (try reading it aloud). Why? Because
speech is, by its nature, usually unstructured, superficial and low
in content.
(Richard McRoberts, *Writing Workshop: A Student's Guide to the
Craft of Writing*, Macmillan, South Melb., Vic., 1981, pp. 4, 5)

In this case the accompanying discussion is more helpful; but there
are still some mistakes along the way. The sample of speech **was** tentative and spur-of-the-moment; but it was not formless. Speech is, by
its nature, 'low in content'—in the special sense of lexical density as
described in Chapter 5 above; but it is not 'low in content' in the general
sense of lacking information; and it is certainly not unstructured and
superficial.

The disorderly
appearance of
speech is an artefact
of the way it is
transcribed.

The 'formlessness' of speech is an artefact of the transcription; if
a written text is reproduced with all the planning processes left in, then
it too will appear formless. But even the most sympathetic transcription will not make spoken language look good in writing, for an obvious
reason: it wasn't meant to be written down. In the same way, most
written English does not sound too good in speech; try reading the following out loud as if it was conversation:

THE DICTIONARY OF WORLD LITERATURE: CRITICISM—
FORMS—TECHNIQUE presents a consideration of critics and
criticism, of literary schools, movements, forms, and techniques—
including drama and the theatre—in eastern and western lands from the
earliest times; of literary and critical terms and ideas; with other
material that may provide background of understanding to all who, as
creator, critic, or receptor, approach a literary or theatrical work.

All the material here included has been written especially for this
volume. Every item is the product of planning, consultation, and
consideration both before and after writing. As far as possible,
especially in the longer articles, the style of every contributor has been
respected. With some of the factual items principally (as in the classical
field) the editor has had to use a freer hand, where a topic was covered
for various periods by different scholars, or presented in detail beyond
the proportioned capacity of this volume. The several problems of cuts
and interlinkings have been met with the work as a whole in mind, in the
effort to combine accuracy and adequacy of presentation with due

proportion and scope. Bibliographies indicate further avenues of inquiry.

The listing of the contributors' names is no measure of their service. (In one or two discussions of current topics, the editor has inserted reference to the authors, who had modestly withheld such mention.) Many have been helpful, beyond any indication of their initials, in the organization of the material as well as in its final shaping. Suggestions have come most generously from Fernand Baldensperger; G.A. Borgese; A.K. Coomaraswamy; Marian Harman; Urban T. Holmes, Jr.; William S. Knickerbocker; Manuel Komroff; J. Craig La Drière; Eliseo Vivas. Allardyce Nicoll has been richly responsive with material concerning the theatre. In addition to contributing therein, William A. Oldfather has supervised the wide range of the classics. Walter A. Reichart has organized and edited the Germanic field.

(From Preface to *Dictionary of World Literature: Criticism, Forms, Technique* ed. J. T. Shipley, Routledge, London 1945, p. v)

Representing one through the lens of the other is rather like judging a painting by whether or not it makes a good photograph.

One has to think of both written and spoken language in terms of three interrelated aspects: the nature of the medium, the functions served, and the formal properties displayed—let us say function, medium, and form:

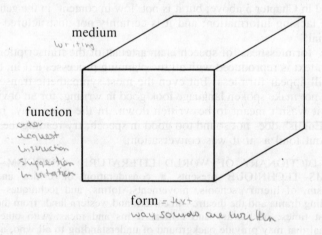

The three go together. So the spoken medium, in which text is a process (and becomes a product only by translation—being 'written down'), displays certain properties of organisation, and is appropriate to certain functions. It can be produced very quickly, make rapid adjustments in the light of the changing context, and express subtle nuances of inter-personal meaning. It tends to be disvalued in written cultures because it is not the primary means of access to power and privilege. But before

78

writing ever existed the spoken language was the vehicle of poetry, oratory, and the sacred; and even in our own culture it has not entirely lost its rhetorical value. At the very least we appreciate a good conversationalist.

The spoken language is, in fact, no less structured and highly organised than the written. It could not be otherwise, since both are manifestations of the same system.

Speech is no less highly organised than writing.

Spoken English and written English are both kinds of English, and the greater part of their patterning is exactly the same. But just as we were able to identify a feature that is particularly found in written English, that of high lexical density, so we can point out a related property that is especially characteristic of the spoken language—one that is not simply the absence of the feature already described.

Spoken English has, in fact, its own kind of complexity, arising out of the nature of the medium. In order to investigate this we shall have to make one further exploration into English grammar, up to the rank of what we are calling the CLAUSE COMPLEX. This is what lies behind the sentence as a written unit; but it does not depend on the written language, and is well developed in the speech of children a long time before they can read or write. The clause complex plays an important part in the processes of oral communication.

Lexical sparsity in spoken language

Let us come back to the notion of lexical density. Here is a comparison between a sentence from a written text and a possible rendering of it in spoken form:

||| The use of this method of control unquestionably leads to safer and faster train running in the most adverse weather conditions. |||

This is a single clause; it contains twelve lexical items, so it would have a lexical density of 12. A typical spoken variant might be:

||| If this method of control is used || trains will unquestionably (be able to) run more safely and faster || (even) when the weather conditions are most adverse |||

Here the same twelve lexical items are distributed among three clauses; density 4.

The second version was still not very colloquial; the aim was to alter the vocabulary as little as possible. A more natural spoken version might go something like the following:

||| You can control the trains this way || and if you do that || you can be quite sure || that they'll be able to run more safely and more quickly [[than they would otherwise]] || no matter how bad the weather gets |||

Here the lexical items are *control*, *trains*, *way*, (not *do*, which is a pro-verb here,) *sure*, *run*, *safely*, *quickly*, *bad*, *weather*, *gets*: ten altogether, including some very common ones. The number of clauses has now risen to five (not counting the embedded one); so the figure for lexical density is down to 2.

But notice how this effect has been achieved. It is not by any significant change in the total number of lexical items. We have abandoned one or two unnecessary ones (*leads to*, *conditions*), and replaced one or two others (*method* by *way*, *adverse* by *bad*); but by and large the vocabulary has remained the same. What has changed is the grammar.

Let us check this by taking a text in spoken English and 'translating' it into writing:

> ||| Or they could be in an aeroplane || and there was a great electrical storm || and they were blown off course || and the electricity made all the radio go dead || so there were no radio sounds || and nobody could hear them |||

Six clauses with thirteen lexical items; lexical density just over 2. Here is a possible 'translation':

> ||| Alternatively they might be in an aeroplane, || which was blown off course by a violent electrical storm; || the electricity silenced the radio, || so that they could no longer be heard |||

Twelve lexical items distributed over four clauses; density 3. Taking a further step in the 'written' direction:

> ||| As a possible alternative, the aeroplane || in which they were travelling || might have been deflected from its course by a violent electrical storm, || which disrupted radio communication || and prevented them from being audible |||

Thirteen lexical items, three clauses—again, omitting the embedded one; density just over 4. (Embedded clauses are not counted separately, since they function inside another clause—if they were counted, then the lexical items inside them would have to be counted twice, as they would be occurring **both** within the embedded clause **and** within the outer clause.)

We shall not continue with the counting—the figures themselves are of no great significance; they are necessary simply to establish the point. On the basis of various samples I have found that a typical average lexical density for spoken English is between 1.5 and 2, whereas the figure for written English settles down somewhere between 3 and 6, depending on the level of formality in the writing. Obviously, the figures themselves will vary considerably according to the theoretical basis of the analysis—criteria for deciding what is a lexical item, and criteria for deciding what is a clause, as well as whether to count only ranking clauses or to include embedded ones. But provided whatever criteria are adopted are applied consistently, the lexical density of written language is likely to be of the order of twice as high as that for speech; and the discrepancy will be greater if other factors such as the relative probability of lexical items are taken into account.

In the next section we shall examine what it is that gives this low lexical density to spoken English.

Representing experience in talk

If we compare pairs of wordings that are paraphrases of each other, one typical of writing, the other typical of speech, we find regular patterns such as the following:

Written	Spoken
Every previous visit had left me with a sense of the futility of further action on my part.	Whenever I'd visited there before, I'd ended up feeling that it would be futile if I tried to do anything more.
Violence changed the face of once peaceful Swiss cities.	The cities in Switzerland had once been peaceful, but they changed when people became violent.
Improvements in technology have reduced the risks and high costs associated with simultaneous installation.	Because the technology has improved it's less risky than it used to be when you install them at the same time, and it doesn't cost so much either.
Opinion in the colony greeted the promised change with enthusiasm.	The people in the colony rejoiced when it was promised that things would change in this way.

The basis of the distinction is this. Written language represents phenomena as **products**. Spoken language represents phenomena as **processes**. And this corresponds to the difference between written and spoken discourse.

Each code represents reality as being like itself. A piece of writing is an object; so what is represented by written language is also given the form of an object. Hence *visit, sense, futility, action, violence, improvements, costs, installation, opinion, change, enthusiasm* are all nouns.

But when you talk, you are doing; so when you represent by talking you say that something happened or something was done. Hence *had visited, had ended up feeling, tried to do, had been, has improved, install, doesn't cost, rejoiced, change* are all verbs.

We can express the same thing from the point of view of the reader or listener. When you read, the text is presented to you synoptically: it exists, spread out on the page. So you are predisposed to take a synoptic view of what it means. Behind it is a tableau—like the pictures from which writing originally evolved. When you listen, the text is presented to you dynamically: it happens, as waves travel through the air. So you are predisposed to take a dynamic view of what it means. Behind it, things are happening—the visual analogue is a film, not a painting.

With modern technology, the distinction is being blurred. We have tape repeaters and transcribing machines that enable us to listen to small chunks of speech, say two to five seconds of it, over and over again, so that it becomes just another kind of **thing**. And on the other hand, with computers, much of our reading matter is now fed to us in the form of moving text, line following line up the screen with only two or three lines visible at a time; here written text has turned into a process.

So the period of our semiotic history which began with the invention of printing in the Tang dynasty in China, and reached Europe just in time for the Renaissance, a period in which speech and writing were pushed very far apart by the application of technology to writing, may now be coming to an end. At least one of the factors that has led to

Speech and writing are two rather different ways of representing our experience.

The distinction between speech and writing is becoming blurred as a consequence of modern technology.

the difference between spoken and written language, the effect of the medium on the message (to hark back to McLuhan's formulation in the 1960s), may now be disappearing; not that the medium will cease to have an effect, but that in both cases—both speech and writing—the nature of the medium itself has begun to change.

This is not, of course, the only factor involved; there are also differences between what tends to be written about and what tends to be spoken about, reflecting the different functions of speech and writing in our culture. But these are changing too. And just as in the past, when new demands are made on language so the language changes in response to them, as in the centuries after the age of Chaucer in English, now that once again we are making language work for us in ways it never had to do before, it will have to become a different language in order to cope. Exactly how this will happen—and whether we need to intervene with some language planning in order to help it to happen—is one of the fascinating problems confronting linguistics today.

The clause complex in spoken language

Meanwhile we need to investigate the consequences, for spoken language, of the fact that it interprets experience for us in the way it does: not as 'action' and 'event' but as 'is doing' and 'is happening'.

It takes a clause to represent experience in the form of a process (action or event, mental process, relation).

To refer to an object takes a noun; but to say that something is happening takes more than a verb—it takes a clause. The immediate reason for this lies in the grammar: verbs do not occur by themselves, except in the kind of clause that is used to demand goods-and-services, where *Catch!* is interpreted as 'you do it now'. In other speech functions, a process in English requires a battery of accompanying features: various associated participants, 'doer', 'done to', 'done for', and so on; a POLARITY—'it is happening', or else 'it isn't happening', or some intermediate stage (known as MODALITY) 'it may be happening'; and a time base. Of course, these features can be added to a noun; but it still remains a nominal group—whereas when they are added to a verb, it becomes a clause:

(an) approach:
their approach to the government
  for possible future assistance.

(to) approach:
they approached the government
  to ask if they might be able to
  help them.

As this example shows, the 'process' form of expression may need not just one clause to match an equivalent 'product' form; it may need two or more. The examples in Chapter 5 above illustrated the same point.

Clauses have to be strung together in meaningful ways.

But a sequence of such clauses cannot simply be strung together. If the matter is being represented as a complex phenomenon, or as a set of interrelated phenomena, then the relationship has also to be brought out. This is the function of the clause complex.

A clause complex is the grammar's way of showing (1) **that** and (2) **how** the processes going together in a sequence are all related to each other. There are essentially two ways of doing this:

1. They can be treated as equal, none being dependent on any other (PARATAXIS)
2. They can be treated as unequal, one being dependent on another (HYPOTAXIS).

These two possibilities arise between any pair of related clauses.

Examples of parataxis are:

Clause 1	Clause 2
It's less risky	and/or/but/so it costs less.
It's quite safe:	there's no danger.
Thomas said,	'There's no danger'.

Examples of hypotaxis are:

Clause α	Clause β
They approached the government	instead of fending for themselves.
They approached the government	who rejected their appeal.
They approached the government	asking/(in order) to ask for a loan.
They said	they would approach the government.

Clause β	Clause α
Instead of fending for themselves,	they approached the government
Because they needed a loan	they approached the government
They would approach the government,	they said.

the clause complex: parataxis and hypotaxis

It will be seen that parataxis and hypotaxis are related to the traditional notions of co-ordination and subordination. But the traditional categories are rather differently defined, so it would be misleading to use these terms. Parataxis includes:

1. (a) 'and/or'-type complexes (traditionally 'co-ordinate')
   (b) 'i.e./e.g.'-type complexes (traditionally a kind of apposition)
   (c) 'then/so/but'-type complexes

2. direct (quoted) speech complexes.

Hypotaxis includes:

1. (a) 'besides/instead of'-type complexes
   (b) 'non-defining relative' complexes
   (c) 'when/because/if'-type complexes

2. indirect (reported) speech complexes

The dependent clause (marked as β in the notation) may be finite or non-finite (whereas non-finite clauses are not recognised in traditional grammar). On the other hand, hypotaxis does **not** include embedding, which is a very different kind of phenomenon. In the following examples:

1. **Have you seen my husband, who came in with me?** (hypotaxis)
2. **Have you seen the man who came in with me?** (embedding)

83

(1) is a **clause complex** consisting of two clauses, structure $\alpha\hat{\ }\beta$. It will be spoken on two tone groups (possibly with a silent beat between); and it is possible to respond to either clause—the listener could reply *Did he?* as well as *I haven't.*

(2) is a single **clause**; it happens to have another one embedded inside it. It will be spoken on one tone group; and it is not possible to respond to the embedded clause—it does not make sense to reply *Did he?*

Combining clause and tone group notation we get the following:

1. |||//2 have you / seen my / **husband** || who //2 came in / **with** me |||//
2. |||//2 have you / seen the / man || who / came in / **with** me || |||//

In mathematical terms, the hypotactic relation is one of iteration, whereas embedding is one of recursion.

Parataxis and hypotaxis are relations between pairs of clauses. A typical clause complex will combine both, for example:

||| Swiss cities had once been peaceful	|| but they changed	|| when people became violent. |||

1	2α	2β
{ 1	$2(\alpha$	$\beta)$}

||| because the technology has improved	|| it's less risky	when you install them	|| and it doesn't cost so much either |||

β	$\alpha1\alpha$	$\alpha1\beta$	$\alpha2$
[β	$\alpha\{1(\alpha$	$\beta)$	2}]

Such sequences can be represented by bracketing, or by repeating the symbols. If the structure is written out in a line, the 'concatenation' symbol (a circumflex) can be used to mark off each symbol complex:

$\beta\hat{\ }\alpha1\alpha\hat{\ }\alpha1\alpha\hat{\ }\alpha2$

Some longer passages of speech

Let us now consider some longer sequences. Here are three passages taken from spontaneous speech by different people talking about their experiences of breeding and showing dogs (recorded by Guenter Plum):

How it actually started was that both my wife and myself were working—she was a secretary at the particular time, I was with a commercial company, commercially travelling; and we liked the Basenji as a breed of dog, but we felt we weren't in a position to own one at the time because we were out normal working days and things like this, and at that particular time we were living in a big home unit but it wasn't what you'd call suitable for a dog, and it was virtually when we got into our own first business, which was contract cleaning, that we decided that we were in a position timewise to look after one.

And I had to wait, I had to wait till it was born and till it got to about eight or ten weeks of age, then I bought my first dachshund, a black-and-tan bitch puppy—as they told me I should have bought a bitch puppy to start off with, because if she wasn't a hundred per cent good I could choose a top champion dog to mate her to and then produce something that was good, which would be in my own kennel prefix.

So we rang up the breeder, and she sort of tried to describe the dog to us, which was very hard to do over the phone, so we went over to have a look to see what they were like, and we bought Sheba, because at that stage Bob was away a lot on semi-trailers with the army and it used to get quite bad with the exercises— you'd have prowlers and perverts through the married quarters, so if we—you know—got a dog, which we could do because it didn't matter what sort of dog anyone had, it'd bark and they wouldn't bother us.

The structure of the last of these was as follows:

so we rang up the breeder	1
and she tried to describe the dog to us	2α
which was very hard to do over the phone	2β
so we went over	3α
to have a look	3β
to see	3γα
what they were like	3γβ
and we bought Sheba	4α
because at that stage Bob was away a lot with the army	4β1
and it used to get quite bad with the exercises	4β21
you'd have prowlers through the married quarters	4β22
so if we got a dog	4β3βα
which we could do	4β3ββα
because it didn't matter what sort of dog anyone had	4β3βββ
it'd bark	4β3α1
and they wouldn't bother us	4β3α2

To show that discourse of this kind is not special to dog fanciers, here are three other extracts: one from a mother helping her daughter with her homework, one from an academic, and one from a child aged 6;4:

The more tests you do, and the more different ways that questions are put to you, the more you're going to understand what the questions are about. So what you're doing is sort of having a big bath of scientific language, and the more times you get into the bath the better you swim. And these kinds of tests are really good, because at school the teacher knows what she's taught you, and she knows the words she's used and everything else; these tests are sort of generalised, so there's no way they can know exactly what you've learnt, but they know approximately what you should be learning about, so they ask you questions to test how much of the information has gone into your brain and been assimilated so that you can reproduce it even if the question is slightly different.

(recorded by Robert Borel de Bitche)

The one comment I'd have has to do with her writing this up. The dissertation was written within the frame 'these are the extant theories; let's use these to derive hypotheses and get some data and cast them against the theories', and that's fine, but it's also a limit, because it leads her for example not to ask such questions as the kind of thing I was pushing her on a little bit, what alternative meanings might be given to the class variable other than the socialization—it is true that in this literature the class variable is interpreted as a socialization variable, but that's not necessarily the case if you start from the more general question of how can we explain radicalism rather than the more particular question of given the theories currently used to explain radicalism. (recorded by Allen Grimshaw)

When we ride on a train in the railway museum it's an old-fashioned train but we call it a new-fashioned train though it's old-fashioned because it's newer than the trains that have only got one.
—One what?
—One driving wheel. But when we ride on a Deltic not in a museum we call it an old-fashioned train.

It is often thought that sequences of conversational discourse like this are simply strings of 'ands'. These extracts make it clear that they are not. Rather, they are intricate constructions of clauses, varying not only in the kind of interdependency (parataxis or hypotaxis) but also in the logical semantic relationships involved. These include not only three basic types of expansion—adding a new point, restating or exemplifying the previous one, or adding a qualification—but also the relationship of projection, whereby the speaker brings in what somebody else says or thinks and incorporates it grammatically into his own discourse.

the clause complex in spoken language: a highly organised structure

The clause complex is the resource whereby all this is achieved. It embodies the fundamental iterative potential of the grammar. This potential is found with words and groups as well as with clauses; for example, the long strings of nouns that we find in headlines, machine part names, and catalogues. But as a particular feature of spoken language its main contribution is at the rank of the clause. The natural consequence of the spoken language's preference for representing things as processes is that it has to be able to represent not one process after another in isolation but whole configurations of processes related to each other in a number of different ways. This is what the clause complex is about.

Two kinds of complexity

It is wrong, therefore, to think of the written language as highly organised, structured, and complex while the spoken language is disorganised, fragmentary, and simple. The spoken language is every bit as highly organised as the written, and is capable of just as great a degree of complexity. Only, it is complex in a different way.

The complexity of the written language is static and dense. That of the spoken language is dynamic and intricate. Grammatical intricacy takes the place of lexical density. The highly information-packed, lexically dense passages of writing often tend to be extremely simple in their grammatical structure, as far as the organisation of the sentence (clause complex) is concerned. Here is a passage from a philosophical work:

> We have defined the content of a scientific discipline by reference to three interrelated sets of elements: (1) the current explanatory goals of the science, (2) its current repertory of concepts and explanatory procedures, and (3) the accumulated experience of the scientists working in this particular discipline—i.e., the outcome of their efforts to fulfil their current explanatory ambitions, by applying the available repertory of concepts and explanatory procedures. So understood, of course, the 'experience' of scientists is not at all the sort of thing assumed, either by sensationalist philosophers like Mach, for whom the ultimate data of science were supposedly 'sense-impressions', or by physicalist philosophers such as the logical empiricists, for whom 'scientific experience' simply comprises straightforward factual generalizations. Rather, the experience of scientists resembles that of other professional men: for example, lawyers, engineers or airline pilots.
> (Stephen Toulmin, *Human Understanding*, vol. 1, Clarendon Press, Oxford, 1972, 175-6)

The **argument** is of course complex; but the sentence grammar is extremely simple. There are some embedded clauses inside the nominal groups, but even taking these into account the passage does not display any of the kind of dynamic complexity that is regularly associated with natural, spontaneous speech. The complexity of the written language is its density of substance, solid like that of a diamond formed under pressure. By contrast, the complexity of spoken language is its intricacy of movement, liquid like that of a rapidly running river. To use a behavioural analogy, the structure of spoken language is of a choreographic kind.

the kind of complexity that is typical of spoken language: 'grammatical intricacy'—a choreographic conception

Of course, much conversation is fragmentary, with speakers taking very short turns; and here the potential for creating these dynamic patterns does not get fully exploited. But the difference is not so great as it might seem, because what happens in dialogue is that the speakers share in the production of the discourse; so that although the grammar does not show the paratactic and hypotactic patterns of the clause complex in the way that these appear when the same speaker holds the floor, some of the same semantic relations may be present across turns. Here are two examples, one of three adult speakers, the other of an adult and a child.

(Three adult speakers)

A: //13 actually I / spent / most of last / **year** being / ill / one way and a / **nother** //

B: // do / tell us about.

A: //1 ‸ I was / bitten by a / **snake** //

C: //1 **ooh** what // 1 **sort** //

A: //1 well I / don't / **know** ex //4 **actly** but it //1 made a / very / deep / **hole** in my //1 **foot** . . and //4 the / anti/**venene** //1 made me / very / ill in / **deed** in //13 fact I've / **heard** / **since** of //13 somebody / **dying** from / anti/**venene** //1 not from the / snake's / **poison** //

C: //1 ‸ well it's the / **serum** / allergy //1 **isn't** it it's //13 usually a / **horse** / serum / **allergy** //

A: //13 yes / **that's** / **right** it //1 **was** a / horse / serum / allergy //

C: //1 **yes** //1 **I've** / got it //1 **too** //

A: //13 don't be / bitten by a / **snake** / **then** //

B: //1 **you've** / got it //1 how do you / know / **you've** / got it //

C: //1 ‸ as a re/sult of con/tracting / **tetanus** by //1 being in/jected a/**gainst** / tetanus //

A: //2 ‸ you / **had** / **tetanus** //

C: //1 **yes** //

A: //1 ‸ and / what / happened / **then** //

C: //4 oh I / went / **rigid** for //3 thirty-six / **hours** and then //4 **fortunately** the ef//1 fect / passed / **off** //

A: //1 ‸ so that / wasn't / **long** e/nough to //4 mean that you / **starved** //

C: //1 **no** the //4 danger isn't / usually star/**vation** it's . . . //1 ‸ it at/tacks the / **respiratory** / system and when //13 **that** / **happens** you //3 no longer / **breathe** and //1 therefore you / **die** in a //1 few / **minutes** //

A: //1 like the ef/fect of the / bite of a / **mamba** you //3 just have / time to / say / ‸ good/ **bye** //

C: //1 ‸ I / haven't been / **bitten** by a / mamba //4 **recently** //

A: //1 no but it / **does** //13 paralyse your / **breathing** appa/**ratus** it //4 doesn't—/ ‸ it's / not / poison in the / bloodstream in the / same / way as with / many / **other** / snake / bites it //1 just has a / **paralysing** ef/fect //

B: //1 where / were you / during those / thirty-six / **hours** then / that you were //1 **rigid** //

C: //1 in / **bed** //

A: //2 ‸ at / **home** //

B: //2 ‸ in your / **own** / **bed** or in a //1 **hospital** / bed //

C: //1 ‸ at / **home** it was a //4 long / time a/ **go** //

B: //1 ‸ but pre/sumably / under super/ **vision** //1 medical super/**vision** //

C: //1 oh / **yes** //1 super/vision / all the / **time** I //1 fell out of a / **car** and was //1 therefore in/jected a/gainst / **tetanus** and //3 then a / few months / **later** I //1 fell off my / **bike** and . . . //4 ‸ sort of / broke / everything I / **could** and they in//1 jected me a/**gain** . . . and //3 ‸ you / shouldn't have /

more than / one in/**jection** //1 every / three / **years** for / tetanus
and so //4 **this** //4 added to the / fact that I was al/lergic to
the / **serum**—. . . //1 ˬ they / used / two / different / kinds
of / **serum** the //4 **first** / time it was a //1 **different** sort of
/ serum which //1 didn't / **hurt** me—/ ˬ //4 meant that I /
both con/tracted / **tetanus** and //1 also came / out in / various
/ **weals** and / things like / that all //1 over my / **body** and
//1 lay / **rigid** for a //1 long / **time** //

A: //5 ˬ it / must have been / **terrifying** for the //4 people a/**round**
you //

C: //4 everybody / **else** was //5 given / **brandy** to sort of //5
get them / **over** it but //4 **I** didn't / get any //

(recorded by Afaf Elmenoufy)

(Nigel at 6;3) (topic: the Rainhill trials for the Liverpool & Manchester
Railway, 1829)

N: //1 what is there / in the / water that / makes you / **sink** //2
ˬ in a / **marsh** //

F: //1 **nothing** it's //4 just / ordinary / **water** //1 ˬ you / **always**
/ sink in / **water** //

N: //1 ˬ but / why / can't you / **swim** in the / **water** //

F: //1 **oh** I //1 **see** //1 ˬ be/cause it / isn't / **deep** e/nough //1
ˬ it's / all mixed / up with / mud and / **weeds** //

N: //1 ˬ but / why / can't you / hold / **on** in the / marsh //1 ˬ
to the / bits of / **land** //

F: //1 ˬ well you / **could** //4 ˬ if you were / sinking / in too /
far //1 ˬ but the / bits of / land / sometimes / sink in / **too** //

N: //2 ˬ but / was / Rainhill / still joined / on to / **England** //2
ˬ by a / bit of / land / far / far a/**way** //

F: //1 **oh** yes //1 Rainhill is / **near** the / marsh //1 near Chat
/ **Moss** //1 ˬ and / Chat / Moss is / all / part of / **England**
//1 ˬ it has / England / all / **round** //

N: //4 ˬ so the / trains / **could** have gone //1 **round** a //1 long
long / **way** //1 ˬ but it would have / been too / **far** //

F: //1 **yes** //1 **right** they //4 **could** have gone / round but it would
have //1 been too / **far** //

N: //1 ˬ because / Rocket was the / fastest / train in the / **world**
//1 ˬ it was the / **only** / train . . . //1 ˬ because in / England
were the / only / trains in the / **world** //1 ˬ they / only / had
/ trains in / **England** be/cause they //1 thought it / would have
/ been too / **frightening** //1 ˬ because the / other / countries
/ thought the / trains would have / terrible / **accidents** and
they would have //1 been too / **fast** / ˬ //1 how / fast did the
/ Rocket / **go** //

F: //1 twenty-nine / miles an / **hour** //

N: //1 ˬ that's / just a/bout / **one** / mile an / hour for //4 **these**
/ days //4 ˬ but for / **those** / days //5 **wow** // ˬ it was . . .

Transcribing spoken texts

Why has it become customary to regard the spoken language as disjointed and shapeless? There seem to be three main reasons for this misunderstanding.

One is that of the value systems of literate cultures, already referred to earlier. In an 'oral' culture (i.e. one without writing; to say 'non-literate' gives too much of a negative flavour), the registers of language which are highly valued, and the highly valued texts within those registers, are, obviously, spoken, since speech is all that there is. Once writing evolves, these texts are written down, because writing is felt to be a more reliable way of preserving them; which means that the value is now transferred to written language, and speech comes to be regarded as transitory and inconsequential.

The second reason is that when people begin to transcribe spoken texts, in the age of tape recorders, they are so taken up with the hesitations and 'false starts' (the 'crossing out' phenomenon in speech), the coughs and splutters and clearings of the throat, that they put them all in as a great novelty, and then judge the text on the basis of their transcription of it. (Anyone who had learnt to listen to language would have been aware of these things without the aid of tape recorders, and they would have come as no great surprise; but unless you are trained as a linguist you are likely to process speech without attending to its sounds and its wordings—very naturally so, since this is what is necessary for survival.) But transcribing these features into writing is rather like printing a written text with all the author's crossings out and slips of the pen, all the preliminary drafting mixed up with the final version—and then saying 'Wow! what a mess'. (Imagine reading out an unedited manuscript in this way to someone who is illiterate—that is exactly the picture he would get of what written language is like.)

The third reason seems to be that when philosophers of language began recording speech they started with academic seminars, because they were easiest to get at: there is a lot of talk, the interactants tend to stay in one place, and they wouldn't object to being recorded, since no great personal secrets were likely to be revealed. But this is just the kind of discourse that is most disjointed, because those taking part are having to think about what they are saying, and work out the arguments as they go along. The ordinary everyday exchanges in the family, the gossip among neighbours, the dialogue-with-narrative that people typically bandy around when sitting together over a meal or at the bar—and also the pragmatic discourse that is engendered when people are engaged in some co-operative enterprise—these tend to be much more fluent and articulated, because the speakers are not having to think all the time about what they are saying.

the importance of transcribing spoken language sensibly and with understanding

If one's aim is to bring out all the features that go into the planning of speech, then it is appropriate to transcribe it that way; this is like making a photocopy of an author's original manuscript of a poem, or preserving all the stages that have gone into children's composition—it is a special research task. But one would not use these documents to represent written language. In the same way, if one wants to understand what spoken language is like (as distinct from having some special research purpose of this kind), one looks for a form of transcription that is informative, in that it incorporates the systematic and meaningful properties of speech that ordinary writing leaves out, but that does not put in all the tacking and the bits of material that were left over in the cutting process.

The following are some of the transcription systems for spoken English that are in current use; the references show where they may be found.

alternative kinds of transcription in current use

1. Survey of English Usage system
   R. Quirk & J. Svartvik, *A Corpus of English Conversation* (Longman, London, 1980).
2. Birmingham Discourse Analysis system
   J. McH. Sinclair & D. Brazil, *Teacher Talk* (Oxford University Press, London, 1982).
3. Bristol Language Development Study system
   G. Wells et al., *Learning through Interaction* (Cambridge University Press, Cambridge, 1981).
4. Conversational Analysis system
   H. Sacks, E.A. Schegloff & G. Jefferson, 'A simplest systematics for the analysing of turn-taking in conversation', *Language*, vol. 50, 1974.
5. Language Development Notation
   L. Bloom, *Language Development: Form and Function in Emerging Grammars* (MIT Press, Cambridge, Massachusetts, 1970).
6. Communication Linguistics system
   K. Malcolm, 'Communication linguistics: A sample analysis', J.D. Benson & W.S. Greaves (ed.), *Systemic Perspectives on Discourse* (Ablex, Norwood, New Jersey, 1984).
7. Systemic-functional system
   M.A.K. Halliday, *A Course in Spoken English: Part 3, Intonation* (Oxford University Press, London, 1970).

The last of these is the one that is being used here. It was originally devised for teaching spoken English to foreign students, but has since been used for a variety of linguistic and educational purposes.

For very many purposes, however, there is nothing wrong with transcribing into ordinary orthography. This is easy to read and avoids making the text look exotic. The important requirement if one does use straightforward orthography is to punctuate the text intelligently. We have emphasised all along that writing is not speech written down, nor is speech writing that is read aloud. But the two are manifestations of the same underlying system; and if the one is being represented through the eyes, or ears, of the other, it is important to use the resources in the appropriate way. If you read written language aloud, you do your best to make it sound meaningful. The same guiding principle applies when you write spoken language down.

Chapter 7
Speaking, writing, and learning

Differences between speech and writing

Talking and writing, then, are different ways of saying. They are different modes for expressing linguistic meanings. To go back to our tri-stratal model of language, from Chapter 2: in language, a network of **meanings** ('semantic' system) is encoded through a network of **wordings** ('lexico-grammatical' system), and the wordings are in turn encoded through a network of **expressions**. The expression, in all cultures, makes use of the medium of **sound** ('phonological' system); in some cultures it also makes use of the **visual** medium ('orthographic' or 'graphological' system).

Can we say, then, that talking and writing are different ways of expressing (saying) the same meanings (things)? The answer we are suggesting must be: yes, and no. Yes, in the sense that the two are alternative 'outputs'—alternative realisations of the meaning potential of language; anything that can be said in writing can also be said in speaking, and vice versa. The two are both **language**; and **language is more important than either**. It is a mistake to become too much obsessed with the medium.

'Language' is more important than either spoken language or written language.

At the same time (and again for the same reason), it is important that we should recognise that there are specific senses in which the answer must be 'no'. It is rather like the principle that what is said in any one human language can also be said in any other. As a general principle, this is true; and it is a fundamental and significant truth: all languages have the same potential for expressing human meanings. But in practice each language has evolved in its own culture; and while every language is equally well adapted to serve the needs of (i.e. express the meanings of) the culture within which it itself developed, it is not so well equipped for expressing the meanings of another culture. Aboriginal languages are not, in fact, equipped to express the semiotics of Western societies—nor are European languages suited to the meaning styles of Aborigines. Each would have to adapt itself in order to meet such different demands.

There is an anology with speech and writing. We could identify three respects in which we would have to qualify the generalisation that spoken language and written language are 'saying the same things':

1. Writing does not incorporate all the meaning potential of speech: it leaves out the prosodic and paralinguistic contributions. There are also certain reciprocal effects: spoken language does not show sentence and paragraph boundaries, or signal the move into direct quotation. But these are different: it is the signals that are missing, not the features themselves.

2. Speech and writing are in practice used in different contexts, for different purposes—though obviously with a certain amount of overlap. This is partly a ritual matter, a form of social convention: such institutions as the application form ('please submit your request in writing, in triplicate'), the office memorandum, and the 'copy for the files' are essentially written language rituals—and will remain so in 'the electronic office of the future', even if no longer in the form of trays and cabinets full of paper. But it is mainly for the reason for which writing evolved in the first place: namely, that there are different functions to which each one is appropriate. To that extent, therefore, they are not saying the same things. The meanings that are expressed in contexts where writing is used are normally not translated into talk. No doubt they could be; but there would be no point in it. We do not go around reading the regulations on the airline ticket aloud. (It is a pity, on the other hand, that we do not go around reading plays or reciting poetry aloud—we might get better sounding poetry if we did.) Similarly we do not write down the household management conversations and service encounters of daily life, which are extremely boring to have to read. Just as in a bilingual culture, the languages are almost always specialised out—to different activities, different topics, different personal relationships: there is no point in having two languages both doing all the same things— so there would be no point in having both speech and writing if the two simply duplicated the functions of each other.

> Are there differences in the meanings expressed by spoken and written language?

3. Thirdly there is the point made in the last chapter: that speech and writing impose different grids on experience. There is a sense in which they create different realities. Writing creates a world of things; talking creates a world of happening. The question arises, then, whether one is in some sense more 'basic', 'nearer to reality' than the other; and if so, which. This is not an easy question, and we shall not solve it here. But it deserves a special—if inevitably very sketchy—section of the discussion to itself.

Grammatical metaphor

Notice that when we 'translate' between speech and writing, certain types of wording frequently turn up. On the written side, we tend to have rather few different verbs; those that occur, apart from *be* and its synonyms (*represent, comprise, form, add up to, constitute*, etc.), are often verbs such as *lead to, cause, follow, allow, derive, cover*, and *include*, which are the names of circumstantial relations:

| applause followed the announcement | 'after the announcement, people applauded' |

this development could lead to a different outcome	'in view of this development, things might turn out differently'
he derived much satisfaction from this discovery	'because of this discovery he was very satisfied'
her speech covered five points	'she spoke about five points'

On the spoken side, we find a greater range of verbs. These verbs are turned by the written version into nouns, many of which are therefore the names of processes, like *applause*, *speech*, *outcome*, and *satisfaction* in the examples just cited. In a 'more spoken' equivalent, *announcement*, *development*, and *discovery* might also appear as verbs:

after they had announced (it), people applauded
in view of what has developed, things might turn out differently
he was very satisfied because he had discovered this

Spoken forms are perhaps 'nearer the bone': 'grammatical metaphor' is a feature of written language.

There is a sense in which the spoken forms appear to be nearer the bone. The written variants have a sort of metaphorical quality about them—except that there is no greater degree of metaphor in their choice of **words**, which are the same in both: *announce/announcement*, *applause/applauded*, *discover/discovery*, and so on. (Members of such pairs are 'the same words' in the sense that they are the same LEXICAL ITEMS, differing only in derivation or inflexion.) The metaphor is in the **grammar**. Something that would typically be represented, given the grammatical system of English, as a verb, has been represented instead as a noun.

Why do we say that such things as 'announcing', 'applauding', 'discovering', 'turning out' would typically be represented as verbs? Because in the **semantics** of English they are processes: somebody is doing something, or something is happening. There is a similar element of grammatical metaphor in what the written versions have as their verbs. If one thing 'followed' another, but both 'things' were in fact events, then in the semantics of English the phenomenon is registered as 'that happened, then this happened': two processes, related to each other in time. The typical way of expressing a time **relationship between processes** in the grammar is by a hypotactic or paratactic clause complex:

after they had announced it, people applauded $\beta\hat{}\alpha$
they announced it, then people applauded $1\hat{}2$

But by the use of a grammatical metaphor, the time relation is encoded by a verb, *follow*; as if there was just one process—a 'thenning'—instead of two—one of announcing and one of applauding.

metaphorical and less metaphorical ways of representing meaning in the grammar

Let us make it quite clear that expressing something metaphorically is intrinsically neither better nor worse than expressing it congruently, or 'literally'. All use of language embodies a great deal of metaphor; there is no reason to suppose that language has ever been without it, since it became language as distinct from protolanguage. One could see certain developments even in protolanguage as being metaphorical, to the extent that they involve a transference of meaning. The question is whether metaphor is involved in the phenomenon we are considering here; and if so, while each will appear as metaphorical if viewed from the standpoint of the other, whether there is reason for regarding either one as the more congruent.

Here, in fact, there **are** grounds for interpreting the variation as metaphorical, in a way that is quite independent of whether it occurs in speech or in writing. That is to say, an example such as:

> The council's proposed replacement of subsidies by a loan is incurring the bitter resentment of the medical profession.

contains a considerable amount of grammatical metaphor, and we can produce various less metaphorical versions of it, such as, for instance,

> Because the council is proposing to lend money instead of giving it, (people who work as) doctors are feeling bitterly resentful. Doctors bitterly resent it that the council is proposing that money should be lent instead of being given.

It makes no difference whether on a particular occasion such a form was written or spoken; the point is that the less metaphorical variants tend to occur in speech and the more metaphorical ones tend to occur in writing. Hence we can say that written language is associated with the use of grammatical metaphor.

At the same time, there are many instances of grammatical metaphor that are just as much associated with speech. Some of them may have been borrowed from writing in the first place; but not necessarily so— and some are particularly characteristic of speech, such as that by which a process is represented by the combination of a lexically 'empty' verb (*have, do, make, take, go, give*) with a noun expressing the event or action: *have a bath, make a mistake, give a growl*, and so on. The same principle is at work here as with other nominalising structures: it is possible to expand nouns more easily than verbs, and to say things like *make the same silly mistake, gave two or three warning growls, have a nice hot bath*, which are not easy to express with the verbs *err, growl*, and *bathe*.

Nevertheless this kind of cross-coding in its more complex forms is particularly characteristic of written language, and is one of the ways it achieves its high lexical density. One point to note about it is that it is difficult for young children to understand. We must distinguish, in this respect, among three different phenomena: generalisation, abstraction, and metaphor, since they are mastered at different times in children's language development.

1. Generalisation: from specific to general. Children have no difficulty with this; as soon as they get into the mother tongue, the fact that they have learnt to name things at all means that they have got the idea of a **class** of things. They have to learn what the exact **boundaries** of the classes are: what is a *clock*, what is a *watch*, what is a *radio* and so on; but the **principle** that words name classes, and that some classes include other classes, is not a problem for them.
2. Abstraction: from concrete to abstract. This comes later; children have difficulty with abstract terms typically up to the age of about five. (An example from Nigel at 4;1. He has told his mother a long story about a double-decker bus; she says 'Those are very interesting observations'. Nigel: 'What did she **meàn** by observations?—there are no double-decker observation **coàches**'. To him an *observation* can only mean an observation coach at the back of a train.)
3. Metaphor: from congruent to metaphorical. This (apart from the

Grammatical metaphor is more characteristic of written than of spoken language.

generalisation, abstraction, and metaphor; their place in language development

95

have a bath type, which have taken over and become the regular spoken form) is unlikely to be mastered until the age of eight or nine. This is the explanation of some of the problems that children have with primary school textbooks, when these employ grammatical metaphors in their writing. A clause such as *tradition dictated the wiping of food with hands* is likely to prove difficult.

In this sense, therefore, written languge tends to be rather more highly coded, more removed from—or less **directly** related to—the categories of our experience. This in turn, if we are literate, affects our perceptions of what the world is like. There is, surely, a relationship between the way our experience is encoded in language and the way we apply that experience (or our interpretation of it) to solving problems. But this is an area about which little is yet known.

Learning through language

Most of what we learn, we learn through language. This is true even of our commonsense knowledge, all that we learn before, and outside of, our schooling; but it is especially true of educational knowledge. Language is so central to the whole of the educational process that its role was never even talked about, since no-one could conceive of education without it.

Traditionally the first task of the school has been to ensure that children can read and write. Once a child is literate, it is assumed that he or she can use written language as a tool for learning, in the same way that he or she has always learnt through spoken language. In fact, until recently it would never have been expressed like that; the spoken language was given little or no recognition in educational thinking, and was certainly not thought of as a vehicle of learning. Even today, though speech has been given a place in the classroom, it is seen more as a skill desirable in itself (the need to be articulate, or 'orate', to get on in life) than as essential equipment for learning other things.

At the same time in their **practice** teachers have always shown recognition of the learning potential of the spoken language, because they have expected their pupils to listen to them. Furthermore they have assigned a certain place to speech in their classroom activities. In part, this has been determined by the pattern of speech roles that the spoken language sets up: it is quicker and more effective to check whether a student knows the answer by asking a question orally in class than by setting a written test every time. But there is more to it than that. Anyone who teaches has a sense of what is communicated by speaking and what is communicated by writing; and the two are not identical. If we start with the general notion of learning through language, then some learning takes place more effectively through the spoken language and some through the written.

Of course, there are individual differences in learning style—some learn more through the ear, others through the eye. And there are differences in teaching style; a teacher may be more at home in one or the other medium. But above and beyond these differences are the different

the importance of spoken language in education

world views that are embodied in speech and writing. Put from the learner's point of view: reading/writing and listening/speaking are different ways of learning **because they are different ways of knowing**.

The written language presents a SYNOPTIC view. It defines its universe as product rather than as process. Whether we are talking about a triangle, the layout of a house, or the organisation of a society, the written language encodes it as a structure or, alternatively, as a chaos—but either way, as a **thing** that **exists**. In principle we can freeze it, attend to it, and take it in as a whole. The cost of this perspective may be some simplifying of the relationship among its parts, and a lesser interest in how it got the way it is, or in where it is going next.

The spoken language presents a DYNAMIC view. It defines its universe primarily as process, encoding it not as a structure but as constructing—or demolishing. In the spoken language, phenomena do not exist; they **happen**. They are seen as coming into being, changing, moving in and out of focus, and as interacting in a continuous onward flow. The cost of this perspective is that we may have less awareness of how things actually are, at a real or imaginary point in time; and a lessened sense of how they stay that way.

We emphasised earlier that these different properties are inherent in spoken and written **language**, in whatever form the text is actually presented to us. It is not because a written text is itself a fixed and static object that it represents things in this way; even if we never saw the text, and only heard it read aloud, it would still have the effect of a piece of written language. Similarly, spoken language is spoken language even if it is presented to us in the form of a transcription, as text in writing. Although the special features of each variety clearly derive in the first place from the medium and the functions it serves, once it has evolved the variety becomes independent of the medium and can be transposed into the other form. We can all learn to talk in written language, and even (though this is harder) to compose conversation.

> speaking and writing as different ways of knowing—and hence different ways of learning

Conclusion

In a literate culture, we tend not to take the spoken language seriously. This is not surprising, since not only has writing taken over many of the high prestige **functions** of language in our society, but also our highly valued **texts** are now all written ones. Written records have replaced oral memories as the repositories of collective wisdom and of verbal art.

Linguistics has played a significant part in sanctifying the written language. It is only after language is written down that it becomes an object accessible to conscious attention and systematic study; so grammar begins with writing, and it codifies the written language. The so-called 'traditional grammar' that came into the 'grammar schools' was a theory of written language.

> Traditional grammar was a theory of written language.

Since in writing we only preserve the final draft, such a grammar gives an idealised picture of what language is like. Furthermore, it tends to be used in a normative way, as an ideal that everyone should strive to attain. And as there are always plenty of people around who cannot attain that ideal—children, dialect speakers, foreigners, the illiterate—it provides a useful means of evaluation, of separating the verbally sophisticated sheep from the ungrammatical goats.

Modern linguistics has tried to redress the balance, by paying attention to spoken language as well as written. There are good reasons of principle for this move. Since language evolved as speech, and is learnt as speech by the individual, we have to study it in its spoken form if we are to understand it properly.

If that was the only reason, the study of spoken language might remain the preserve of the linguist, leaving others to devote their attentions to written language as they always have done. But it is not.

There are at least two other reasons for taking the spoken language seriously. One is that it is now coming back into its own as a bearer of cultural value. We have passed the peak of exclusive literacy, where only written artefacts had merit, and information resided only in the written message. (The critical step was probably the invention of the telephone.) Speech has regained at least some of its value in the culture.

The other reason, and no less important, is that referred to in the last section: that we learn by listening and speaking, as well as by reading and writing. Learning is essentially a process of constructing meanings; and the cognitive component in learning is a process of constructing **linguistic** meanings—semantic systems and semantic structures. These systems of meaning, the ideational and interpersonal realities that we create in and through language, embody, as we have seen, two complementary perspectives: the synoptic and the dynamic. When we learn anything, we construe it simultaneously as a universe of things and as a universe of processes—doing and happening. We can think of this most easily in relation to a piece of machinery: in order to understand a machine, we need a synoptic view of its construction as an organic whole, out of parts and parts of parts, and we need a dynamic view of what it performs and how it works. But the same is true of our understanding of anything else, whether of throwing stones in the water or of the family relationships into which we have got ourselves born.

Spoken and written language are adapted to these two dimensions of experience—in the threefold way in which language constructs our world. Language is, at one and the same time, (1) a part of reality, (2) an account of reality, and (3) an image of reality. Let us see how this works out with speaking and writing.

Language and reality: language is at once a part of, an account of, and an image of, the world we live in.

1. Obviously speaking and writing, and their counterparts listening and reading, are both part of reality, in the sense that (once we become literate, at least) both enter into our experience. We are, ourselves, speakers and writers, and verbal activity is just one among the whole range of activities that we engage in.

2. But when we do engage in verbal activity, it is different in kind from other forms of activity in that it unavoidably makes reference to other, non-verbal aspects of our experience. In this sense language is an account of reality; and again this is true of both speaking and writing.

3. If we ask how language is like reality, however, then we find that spoken and written language resemble reality in two different ways.

98

Each is a metaphor for a different dimension of experience. Spoken language happens; it is like the working of the machine, the performance of stones in air and water, the behaviour of fathers and aunts. Written language exists; it is like the machine itself, the stone and the surface of the water, the male and female persons in the environment. And, as we noted, the **forms** of spoken and written language proclaim the metaphor: spoken language favours the clause, where processes take place, whereas written language favours the nominal group, the locus of the constitution of things.

From (3) there is feedback into (2). Because spoken language is an image of the dynamic aspect of reality, so in its account of reality it highlights that aspect—it gives a good picture of how things work. Hence, for example, spoken instructions are usually easier to follow, provided they are timed to fit the task; whereas written instructions often have to be accompanied (or even replaced) by pictures. Written language, on the other hand, highlights the synoptic aspect; it can give a more effective account of the finished product.

Neither the blind nor the deaf need be denied access to either mode—though the linguistic experience of these two groups is totally different. A blind child learns spoken language in the normal way; what he or she needs is a rich enough range of tactile and auditory experience to provide referents for the linguistic forms. For the written medium, moving the touch across sequences of text in braille is closely homologous to scanning writing with the eye, so there is no call to modify the forms of the written language itself.

special linguistic needs of the blind and the deaf

The situation with regard to the deaf is more complex. In sum, the nearest analogue to spoken language in the experience of a deaf child is sign. This is the technical name for the naturally evolving language of deaf communities; the Australian form of it is called AUSLAN. Functionally, it serves the normal purposes of a first spoken language. Formally, it is quite distinct; the use of hand and arm movements, to be looked at, rather than tongue and lip movements, to be listened to, means that the 'wording', or lexico-grammatical system, is significantly different from that of spoken language. But it is a fully functional 'mother tongue', a tri-stratal system that is in no way impoverished; what it lacks in one respect, it makes up in another. A deaf child brought up on sign has to make a greater leap when learning to read and write; not that he or she is less well equipped to cope with written language as such, but that his or her native 'spoken' language is further away from the wordings of written English. One of the approaches to this problem is the use of 'signed English'—English wordings expressed in gestural form. We cannot pursue these issues here; but it is important to stress that the special problems of the deaf are not intrinsic to language (provided that a deaf child of hearing parents has access to sign). They are problems of adequate provision for their specific needs, of communication with the rest of the community, and of the attitudes that others have towards them.

I have tried here to put spoken and written language in perspective relative to each other. In a non-literate society, spoken language performs all the functions that language is called upon to serve; and there is nothing lacking. In a literate society, the functions of language are shared out between speaking and writing; there is some overlap, but by and large they fill different roles.

They are both forms of a language; it is the same linguistic system underlying both. But they exploit different features of the system, and gain their power in different ways.

The idea that spoken language is formless, confined to short bursts, full of false starts, lacking in logical structure, etc. is a myth—and a pernicious one at that, since it prevents us from recognising its critical role in learning. It arises because in writing people only ever analyse the finished product, which is a highly idealised version of the writing process; whereas in speech they analyse—indeed get quite obsessed with—the bits that get crossed out, the insertions, pauses, the self-interruptions, and so on. If we treat that as the norm for speech, then the norm for writing should be as in Figure 7.1.

The powers of spoken and written language complement each other.

Figure 7.1   Written language

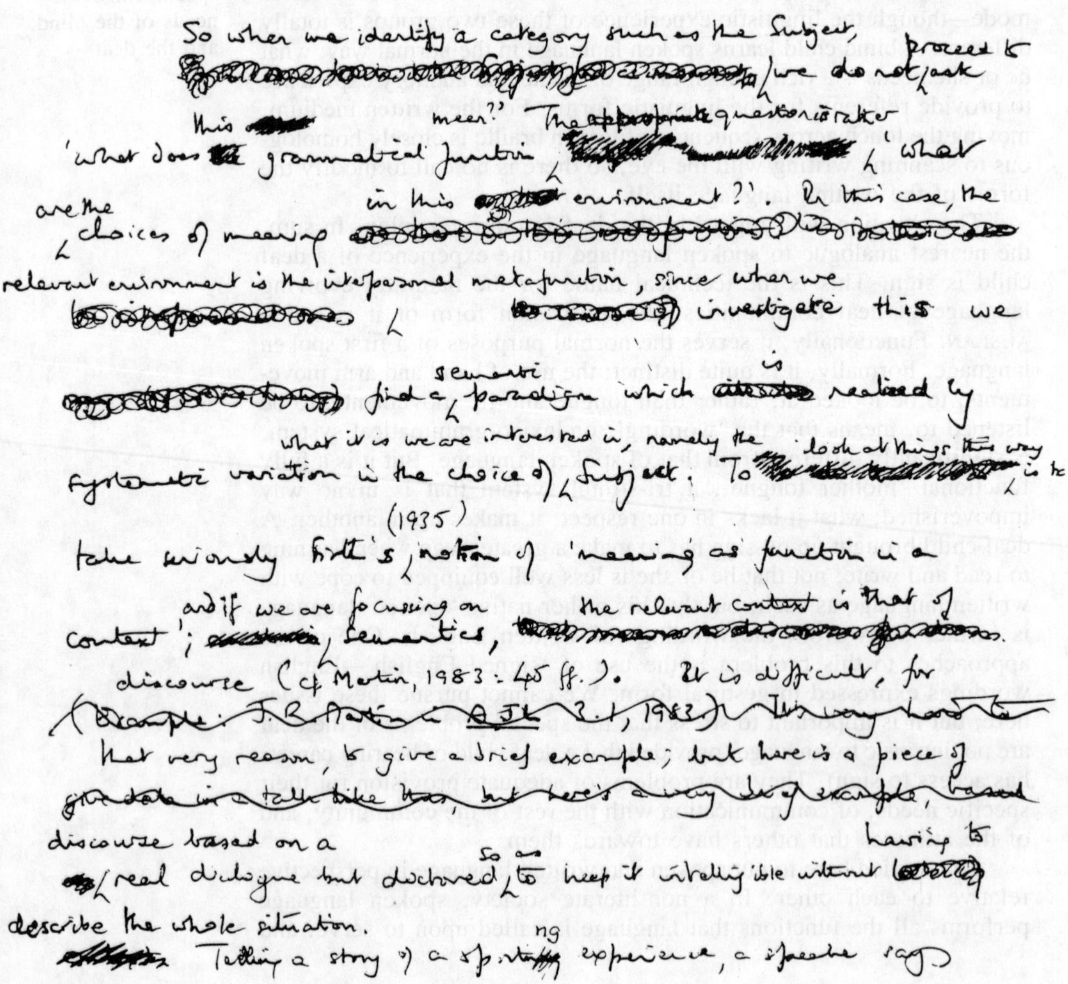

So when we identify a category such as the Subject, we do not ask this ~~mean?~~ The question is rather 'what does the grammatical function ~~~~, 'what are the choices of meaning ~~~~ in this ~~~~ environment?'. In this case, the relevant environment is the interpersonal metafunction, since when we ~~~~ investigate this we ~~~~ find a semantic paradigm which is realized by what it is we are interested in, namely the systematic variation in the choice of, Subject. To look at things this way is to (1935) take seriously Firth's notion of 'meaning as function in a context'; and if we are focussing on semantics, the relevant context is that of discourse (cf Martin, 1983: 45 ff.). It is difficult, for that very reason, to give a brief example; but here is a piece of discourse based on a real dialogue but doctored so as to keep it intelligible without having to describe the whole situation. Telling a story of a spoken experience, a speech ...

Instead of that, however, we do the spoken language—or rather the speaker—the elementary courtesy of taking the finished version as the text. (The intonation and rhythm leave us in little doubt which that is; after all, the listener always knows, and if the person analysing a text cannot even interpret it as well as the listener did he may as well pack up and go home.) This is not, of course, a matter of politeness; it is a matter of understanding. If we persist in treating speech as a caricature of itself, while putting writing (like an inscription) on a pedestal, then there is no way we will ever come to understand how it is that a human child is able to learn.

Appendix A
Special symbols

Grammatical symbols

‖	sentence (clause complex) boundary
∣	clause boundary
∣	group or phrase boundary
⟦ ⟧	embedded clause
[ ]	embedded group or phrase
⟪⟫	inclosed clause
⟨ ⟩	inclosed group or phrase
123 ...	paratactic complex
αβγ ...	hypotactic complex
x^y	'x is followed by y'

Prosodic symbols

//	tone group boundary
/	foot boundary
bold	tonic prominence (information focus)
ˆ	silent beat
1	tone 1 (falling tonic)
2;2	tone 2 (rising tonic; preceded by high fall)
3	tone 3 (level, low rising tonic)
4	tone 4 (falling-rising tonic)
5	tone 5 (rising-falling tonic)
13	tone 13 (1 followed by 3)
53	tone 53 (5 followed by 3)

Phonetic symbols

[ ]	(enclose phonetic transcription)
/ /	(enclose phonemic transcription)

Note: IPA symbols are taken from those on accompanying chart

The international phonetic alphabet
(Revised to 1951)

CONSONANTS	bi-labial	labio-dental	dental and alveolar	retroflex	palato-alveolar	alveolo-palatal	palatal	velar	uvular	pharyngal	glottal
plosive	p b		t d	ʈ ɖ			c ɟ	k g	q ɢ		ʔ
nasal	m	ɱ	n	ɳ			ɲ	ŋ	N		
lateral fricative			ɬ ɮ								
lateral non-fricative			l	ɭ			ʎ				
rolled			r						ʀ		
flapped			ɾ	ɽ					ʀ		
fricative	ɸ β	f v	θ ð s z	ʂ ʐ	ʃ ʒ	ɕ ʑ	ç ʝ	x ɣ	χ ʁ	ħ ʕ	h ɦ
frictionless continuants and semi-vowels	w ɥ	ʋ	ɹ				j (ɥ)	(w)			

VOWELS	Front	Central	Back
close	i y	ɨ ʉ	ɯ u
half-close	e ø		ɤ o
half-open	(ɛ œ)	ə	ʌ ɔ
open	(a)	æ ɐ	ɑ ɒ

References

Abercrombie, D., *Studies in Phonetics and Linguistics*, Language and Language Learning 10 (Oxford University Press, London, 1965).

Boas, F., *Introduction to the Handbook of American Indian Languages* (Georgetown University Press, Washington, DC originally published 1911).

Dixon, R.M.W., *The Languages of Australia* (Cambridge University Press, Cambridge).

Goody, J., *The Domestication of the Savage Mind* (Cambridge University Press, Cambridge, 1968).

Halliday, M.A.K., *Intonation and Grammar in British English*, Janua Linguarum Series Practica 48, (Mouton, The Hague, 1967).

Halliday, M.A.K., *An Introduction to Functional Grammar* (Edward Arnold, London, Baltimore & Melbourne, 1985).

Leakey, R.E., & Roger, L., *People of the Lake: Mankind and its Beginnings* (Doubleday (Anchor Books), Garden City, New Jersey, 1979).

McLuhan, M., *The Gutenberg Galaxy: The Making of Typographic Man* (University of Toronto Press, Toronto, 1962).

Ong, W.J., *Orality and Literacy: The Technologizing of the Word*, New Accents Series (Methuen, London, 1982).

Steele, J., *An Essay towards Establishing the Melody and Measure of Speech, to be Expressed and Perpetuated by Peculiar Symbols* (n.p., London, 1775).

Sweet, H., *A New English Grammar, Logical and Historical, Part II: Syntax* (Clarendon Press, Oxford, 1898).

Trevarthen, C., 'Secondary intersubjectivity: Confidence, confiding and acts of meaning in the first year', in A. Lock (ed.), *Action, Gesture and Symbol: The Emergence of Language* (Academic Press, New York, 1978).

Trevarthen, C., 'Communication and co-operation in early infancy: A description of primary intersubjectivity', in M. Bullowa (ed.), *Before Speech: The Beginning of Interpersonal Communication* (Cambridge University Press, Cambridge, 1979), pp. 321–47.

Further reading

Abercrombie. D., *Studies in Phonetics and Linguistics*, Language and Language Learning 10 (Oxford University Press, London, 1965).

Albrow, K. H., *The Rhythm and Intonation of Spoken English* Nuffield Programme in Linguistics & English Teaching, Paper 9, (Longman, London, 1968).

Christie, F., 'Learning to write: A process of learning how to mean', *English in Australia*, vol. 66, 1983, pp. 4–17.

Collerson, J., 'Discovering what writing is for', in *Children Writing: Reader*, ECT418 Language Studies (Deakin University, Victoria, 1984), pp. 48–53.

Gregory, M., 'Aspects of varieties differentiation', *Journal of Linguistics*, vol. 3, no. 2, 1967, pp.177–98.

Halliday, M. A. K., *Grammar, Society and the Noun*, H. K. Lewis (for University College London), 1967. Reprinted in *Aims and Perspectives in Linguistics*, Occasional Papers 1 (Applied Linguistics Association of Australia, Melbourne, 1977).

Halliday, M. A. K., 'Differences between spoken and written language: Some implications for literacy teaching', in G. Page, J. Elkins & B. O'Connor (eds.), *Communication Through Reading: Proceedings of the Fourth Australian Reading Conference*, vol. 2. (Australian Reading Association, Adelaide, 1979), pp. 37–52.

Mackay, D., Thompson, B., & Schaub, P., *Breakthrough to Literacy Teacher's Manual: Illustrated Edition* (Longman (for the Schools Council), London, 1978).

Trevarthen, C., 'Secondary intersubjectivity: Confidence, confiding and acts of meaning in the first year', in A. Lock (ed.), *Action, Gesture and Symbol: The Emergence of Language* (Academic Press, New York, 1978).

Ure, J. N., 'Lexical density and register differentiation', in G. E. Perren & J. L. M. Trim (eds.), *Applications of Linguistics: Selected Papers of the Second International Congress of Applied Linguistics* (Cambridge University Press, Cambridge, 1971), pp. 443–52.

Scripts and writing systems

Diringer, D., *The Alphabet: A Key to the History of Mankind* (Hutchinson, London 1948. (Third edition (revised, with Reinhold Regensburger), 2 vols, 1968).

Gelb, I. J., *A Study of Writing: The Foundations of Grammatology* (University of Chicago Press, Chicago, 1952).

Registers (functional varieties of language)

Benson, J. D. & Greaves, W. S., *You and Your Language* (Pergamon, Oxford, 1984).

Martin, J. R., 'Language, register and genre', in *Children Writing: Reader*, ECT418 Language Studies (Deakin University, Victoria 1984), pp. 21-30.

Ure, J. N., *An Introduction to Systemic Grammar and its Application to the Study of Register in Contemporary English* (Allen & Unwin, London, 1984).

Written language in school

Martin, N., et al., *Writing and Learning Across the Curriculum 11-16* (Ward Lock Educational, London, 1976).

Thornton, G., *Teaching Writing: The Development of Written Language Skills*, Explorations in Language Study (Edward Arnold, London, 1980).

Writing development

Kress, G. R., *Learning to Write* (Routledge & Kegan Paul, London, 1982).

Martin, J. R. & Rothery, J., *Writing Project Reports 1 & 2*, Working Papers in Linguistics (Department of Linguistics, University of Sydney, 1980/81).

Introduction to linguistics

Chao, Y. R., *Language and Symbolic Systems* (Cambridge University Press, Cambridge, 1968).

Robins, R. H., *General Linguistics: An Introductory Survey*, 3rd edn (Longman, London, 1980).

Early language development

Ede, J. & Williamson, J., *Talking, Listening and Learning: The Development of Children's Language* (Longman, London, 1980).

Halliday, M. A. K., *Learning How to Mean: Explorations in the Development of Language*, Explorations in Language Study (Edward Arnold, London, 1975).

106

Painter, C., *Into the Mother Tongue*, Open Linguistics Series (Frances Pinter, London, 1984).

Some collected papers

Goody, J. (ed.), *Literacy in Traditional Societies* (Cambridge University Press, Cambridge, 1968).

Hodge, B. et al. (eds.), *Readings in Language and Communication for Teachers* (Longman Cheshire, Melbourne, 1983).

Olson, D. R. (ed.), *Social Foundations of Language and Thought* (Norton, New York, 1980).

Tannen, D. (ed.), *Spoken and Written Language: Exploring Orality and Literacy*, Advances in Discourse Processes 9 (Ablex, Norwood, New Jersey, 1982).

Technical terms

Acknowledgements

The author and publishers would like to thank the following for permission to reproduce the material below:

p. 13 *Governor Davey's Proclamation to the Aborigines 1816*, lithograph (hand col.) 47.3×29cm, Rex Nan Kivell Collection NK 458, Artist unknown, National Library of Australia. Reprinted by permission.

pp. 20 and 21 Figures 2.5a and 2.5b from D. Diringer, *The Alphabet*, vol. 2, 3rd edn, Century Hutchinson, London, 1968, pp. 40, 41. Reprinted by permission.

p. 76 extract from G. Beattie, *Talk: An Analysis of Speech and Non-verbal Behaviour in Conversation*, Open University, Milton Keynes, n.d., p. 33. Reprinted by permission.

p. 77 extract from R. McRoberts, *Writing Workshop: A Student's Guide to the Craft of Writing*, Macmillan, Sth Melbourne, 1981, pp. 4, 5. Reprinted by permission.

p. 77 extract from *Dictionary of World Literature*, ed. J. T. Shipley, Philosophical Library Inc., New York, n.d., p.v. Reprinted by permission.